W9-CDF-259

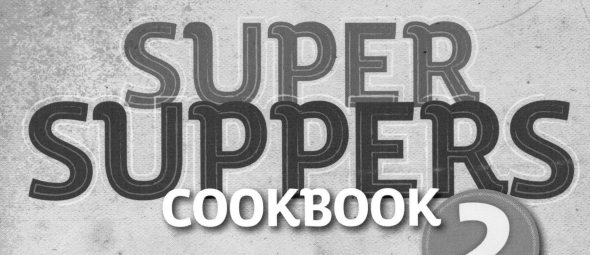

SUPER SUPPERS COOKBOOK 2

Meredith® Books
Des Moines, Iowa

Copyright© 2008 by Judie Byrd

All rights reserved. No part of this book may be reproduced in any form
without written permission from the publisher.

Meredith Books
1716 Locust St.
Des Moines, Iowa 50309–3023
meredithbooks.com

First Edition. Printed in the United States of America.
Library of Congress Control Number: 2008924202
ISBN-13: 978-0-696-24180-2

To moms and dads everywhere who are striving to bring their families back to the dinner table. May these recipes help you make this happen.

Thanks to all the parents who loved our first *Super Suppers Cookbook* and asked for another. And thanks to their families for loving Super Suppers and helping us become the leader in the take-and-bake industry.

Thanks to our wonderful franchisees, who work tirelessly to offer delicious, family-friendly meals that save parents time and energy and alleviate the stress of meal planning and preparation. They solve the age-old dilemma: "What's for dinner?"

Thanks to our Super Suppers staff, who keep our offices running smoothly while maintaining incredibly sweet spirits. With an office full of moms, tasters and testers abound, and this is an enormous help.

I am blessed with dear friends who always cheer me on and give encouragement and support. They also generously share great recipes that have worked for their families.

Thanks to my husband, Bill, who, after 43 years of marriage, is still my rock and giant oak and my best taste-tester! And to our three kids, who have produced a happy, laughing flock of Byrds. Without the kids and grandkids, weekly Family Night, where recipes are practiced and dishes refined, just wouldn't be the same. Thanks to Teresa, Dave, Taylor, Steven, Brian, Stephanie, Allison, Austin, Wyatt, David, and Ceara.

My agent, Leslie Nunn Reed, is an incredible blessing to Bill and me. She is wise, knowledgeable, and understanding, and we appreciate her immensely.

The Meredith team just gets better and better! I am so grateful for the creative insight of editors Tricia Laning and Jennifer Darling. My thanks also goes to art designer Som Inthalangsy for producing a beautiful cookbook that I hope will inspire many families.

contents

a note from JUDIE

When I first began teaching cooking classes in my home 23 years ago, my students would tell me how challenging it was to prepare nutritious suppers night after night. They wanted to bring their families together around the dinner table but felt frustrated and ill-equipped to plan a variety of meals that would nurture and satisfy their busy families.

My heart went out to them. They sensed that this dinnertime routine had value—beyond just the food on the plates. And they were right. Recent research shows that families eating together is "the single strongest predictor of whether adolescents will be well-adjusted." Studies conducted by the National Center on Addiction and Substance Abuse at Columbia University show that teens who have dinner with their families five or more times a week have a 45 percent chance of not trying alcohol, are 32 percent likelier never to have tried cigarettes, and are 24 percent less likely to ever smoke pot. They are twice as likely to get A's in school as classmates who rarely eat with their families.

And then there are the health statistics. The *Journal of Adolescent Health* states that family meals and parental presence at meals is associated with higher intake of fruits, vegetables, and dairy products. The *Wall Street Journal* reports: "Several studies show that kids and adults ingest more calories when eating in front of the TV or at the movies, possibly because the distraction makes us less aware that we're full. Food eaten on the go tends to be high in calories."

So we know the benefits of gathering together as a family each night for dinner are enormous! This is the driving force behind our Super Suppers franchises—to make it easy for moms and dads to pick up family-friendly meals and take them home to bake fresh in their kitchens. There is nothing like a hot, delicious meal coming from your oven, stovetop, or backyard grill. At Super Suppers, you can pick up the entire meal, from entrée, bread, salad and sides, to luscious desserts.

And now, I am excited to share with you more recipes for easy-to-prepare meals. These recipes are satisfying, easy to prepare, and time-sensitive. Some are for foods I raised my kids on, others are from my childhood, and a few are from friends and family. To make life easier, I've given dozens of plan-ahead and freeze-ahead directions. And we've added a chapter to help you plan special events so you can invite friends, family, and neighbors into your home for a shared meal. There's nothing like gathering for home cooking.

I hope you enjoy this cookbook from Super Suppers, and I hope it helps you bring your family back to the dinner table.

Judie Byrd

TIPS, METHODS & TECHNIQUES

Because this book is about making life easier, I've gathered helpful information for you about various staples and simple cooking methods and preparation techniques that we use in the *Super Suppers Cookbook 2* recipes.

FREEZING FOOD: Use freezer bags or cover food with two layers of plastic wrap and one layer of foil. Most food keeps well frozen for up to 2 months.

MELTING CHOCOLATE OVER SIMMERING WATER: Place chocolate chips (if using a block of chocolate, chop it into small pieces) in a stainless-steel bowl and place over a saucepan of simmering water. Stir until most of the chocolate is melted. Remove bowl from heat and continue stirring until smooth.

MINCING/GRATING FRESH GINGER: A whole piece of fresh ginger is called a hand. Break off the "fingers" and use a carrot peeler to remove the peel. Use a small grater to grate the amount you need. To store fresh ginger, peel and place in a jar; pour vodka to cover. Cover jar and refrigerate indefinitely.

PEELING AND DEVEINING SHRIMP: With both hands, grasp the feelers on underside of shrimp and peel away from the body. Use a small knife to slit along the back and pull out the tiny vein.

PEELING TOMATOES: Bring a saucepan of water to a boil. Add tomatoes to boiling water for 10 to 20 seconds (this cooks the outer skin), then remove to a bowl of ice water (this stops the cooking process). Use a paring knife to peel away the skin.

ROASTING BELL PEPPERS: Place bell pepper on a baking sheet and place under broiler. Roast pepper until it chars on one side. Use tongs to turn the pepper, and char the other side. Keep turning the pepper until all sides are charred. Remove pepper and wrap in a paper towel for 5 minutes. Remove the stem and inside membranes from the pepper and peel it. Now it is ready to use.

SIMMERING: A cooking method that calls for food to be covered or partially covered in water or other liquid that is heated on the stovetop, and kept at just below the boiling point. A simmering liquid should produce movement, but not a lot of bubbles as in a boiling liquid.

TOASTING NUTS OR SESAME SEEDS: Preheat oven to 350°F. Spread nuts or sesame seeds on baking sheet. Sesame seeds need to bake only 3 to 4 minutes or just until they begin to brown. Bake nuts from 4 to 8 minutes, tossing halfway through. Toast extra seeds or nuts and freeze in freezer bag or covered jar. They are great for throwing into tossed salads.

ZESTING LEMON AND ORANGES: When using the zest or peel of citrus fruit, use only the colored, outermost layer. This is where the flavorful oils are. Use a grater such as a fine Microplane®. Rub the fruit only once in any one spot to avoid including the pith, which tends to be bitter.

BRAISE (BRAYZ) To cook food by first browning in fat, then adding liquid, covering, and cooking slowly over low heat, either on the stovetop or in the oven. Used to tenderize tough cuts of meat and develop flavors through a long cooking time.

CAPERS Buds from a Mediterranean shrub that are cured in salt and vinegar. Used as a condiment (with dishes such as smoked salmon) or as a flavoring in many Mediterranean recipes.

CARAMELIZE The process of slowly cooking foods until their sugars turn brown and flavorful.

CHINESE FIVE-SPICE POWDER A spice blend that comes in a bottle and generally includes ground cinnamon, cloves, fennel seeds, star anise, and peppercorns.

CORNISH GAME HENS Miniature chickens, a cross between Cornish and White Rock chickens, weighing up to 2½ pounds each.

COUSCOUS (KOOS-KOOS) A North African pasta shaped like tiny spheres.

CREOLE SEASONING A prepared blend of spices and herbs used to flavor Creole cooking, a New Orleans cooking style combining elements of African, French, and Spanish cuisines.

CUMIN (KYOO-MIHN) Also known as comino. This spice is made from the dried seeds of a type of parsley plant and has a deep, nutty flavor. Used in Middle Eastern and Mexican cooking.

DUTCH OVEN A large, squat kettle with a lid, used for stewing and braising.

EN PAPILLOTE (AHN PA-PEE-YOHT) A French cooking method in which food is wrapped in parchment paper or foil.

FLAT-LEAF PARSLEY Also known as Italian or French parsley, it has dark, flat leaves. It is preferred over curly parsley in cooking because of its smoother texture.

FOOD MILL A kitchen tool that mashes food by pressing it through a strainer. The food is moved through the strainer by a hand-cranked paddle.

KALAMATA OLIVES (KAHL-UH-MAH-TUH) Dark Greek olives that are brined in vinegar and olive oil.

KIELBASA (KIHL-BAH-SAH) Fully cooked, smoked Polish link sausage, usually made from pork.

NAPA CABBAGE Mild-flavored Chinese cabbage with large, elongated heads and tightly packed, cream-colored leaves that turn light green on the tips.

ORZO (OHR-ZOH) Rice-shaped pasta.

SAUTÉ (SAW-TAY) To cook food quickly in a skillet-type pan over high heat, using a small amount of fat.

SHALLOT (SHAL-UHT; SHUH-LOT) A small, purple onion that, like garlic, is composed of cloves instead of layers. Its subtle flavor makes it ideal for seafood dishes.

beef

Meatloaf with Apple Glaze

KETCHUP, APPLES, AND HORSERADISH CREATE A FABULOUS SWEET-SOUR FLAVOR. THE APPLE GLAZE "GILDS THE LILY."

SIDES: Cheesy Corn Casserole (page 167) and tossed green salad.

DESSERT: Quick Fruit Crisp (page 177).

MAKES 8 to 10 servings

Nonstick cooking spray

- 2 **pounds ground beef**
- 1½ **cups herb-seasoned stuffing mix, crushed**
- ½ **cup finely chopped onion**
- 1 **large apple, peeled, cored, and finely chopped**
- 3 **large eggs, lightly beaten**
- 1¼ **cups ketchup**
- 2 **tablespoons Dijon mustard**
- 1 **tablespoon horseradish**
- 2 **teaspoons salt**
- 1 **12-ounce can frozen apple juice concentrate, thawed**
- ½ **cup chicken broth**
- 2 **teaspoons Chinese five-spice powder**

ONE Preheat oven to 350°F. Coat a 13x9x2-inch baking pan with cooking spray; set aside.

TWO In a large bowl combine ground beef, stuffing mix, onion, apple, eggs, ¾ cup of the ketchup, the mustard, horseradish, and salt. Form into a loaf in the prepared pan.

THREE Bake 1½ hours or until internal temperature registers 155°F on an instant-read thermometer.

FOUR Meanwhile, make apple glaze. In a saucepan combine apple juice concentrate, broth, five-spice powder, and the remaining ½ cup ketchup. Simmer for 10 to 15 minutes or until reduced to a thick glaze. Top meatloaf with apple glaze the last 5 minutes of baking. Let stand 10 minutes before slicing.

PLAN AHEAD: Prepare recipe through Step Two except do not preheat oven. Cover and refrigerate up to 1 day. Continue according to Step Three.

FREEZE AHEAD: Prepare recipe through Step Four. Cover and freeze up to 2 months. Defrost completely in refrigerator. Reheat in a 350°F oven for 30 minutes or until heated through. Let stand 10 minutes before slicing.

Mom's Shortcut Meatloaf

SIMPLE AND SURE, THIS RECIPE HAS SERVED ME WELL FOR YEARS.

SIDES: Tomatoes Stuffed with Creamed Spinach (page 161) and Arizona Potatoes (page 166).

DESSERT: Frozen Banana Split Pie (page 189).

MAKES 4 servings

Nonstick cooking spray

1   pound ground beef

1   1- to 1½-ounce envelope onion soup mix

½   cup tomato sauce

½   cup ketchup

ONE Preheat oven to 350°F. Coat a 13x9x2-inch baking pan with cooking spray; set aside.

TWO In a large bowl combine ground beef, soup mix, and tomato sauce. Shape into a loaf in the prepared pan.

THREE Spread top of meatloaf with ketchup. Bake 1 hour or until internal temperature registers 155°F on an instant-read thermometer. Let stand 10 minutes before slicing.

PLAN AHEAD: Prepare recipe through Step Two except do not preheat oven. Cover and refrigerate up to 2 days. Continue according to Step Three.

FREEZE AHEAD: Prepare recipe through Step Two except do not preheat oven. Cover and freeze up to 1 month. Defrost completely in refrigerator. Preheat oven. Spread meatloaf with ketchup. Bake according to Step Three.

NOTE: This meatloaf doubles easily.

Taco Pie

TO MAKE THIS DINNER LOOK FESTIVE AND FUN, SPREAD THE CORN CHIPS ON A LARGE PLATTER AND ARRANGE THE REMAINING INGREDIENTS IN LAYERS, ALLOWING EACH LAYER TO SHOW SOME OF ITS COLOR. LARGE PLATTERS MAKE FOOD LOOK IMPRESSIVE AND DELICIOUS.

SIDE: Corn and Black Bean Salad with Chili-Lime Dressing (page 150).

DESSERT: Chocolate ice cream topped with sliced bananas and marshmallow cream.

MAKES 6 servings

1   **pound ground beef**

2   **tablespoons taco seasoning mix (or to taste)**

1   **12-ounce bag corn chips**

    Chopped lettuce

    Chopped onion

    Chopped tomatoes

1   **cup shredded cheddar cheese**

    Taco sauce

ONE In a large skillet cook ground beef until meat is brown. Drain off fat. Stir in taco seasoning.

TWO Spoon meat over corn chips and top with lettuce, onion, tomatoes, and cheese. Serve with taco sauce.

PLAN AHEAD: Prepare recipe through Step One. Cover and refrigerate up to 2 days. Reheat over medium-low heat. Continue according to Step Two.

FREEZE AHEAD: Prepare recipe according to Step One. Cover and freeze up to 1 month. Defrost completely in refrigerator. Reheat over medium-low heat. Continue according to Step Two.

OPTION: Chicken Taco Pie: Toss 2 cups cooked, chopped chicken with the taco seasoning; omit ground beef.

That'sa Quick and Easy Meatballs

SERVE OVER PASTA OR RICE, OR PILE ONTO HOAGIE BUNS AND TOP WITH CHEESE FOR GREAT SANDWICHES.

SIDES: Pasta or rice and Sautéed Spinach and Pine Nuts (page 157).

DESSERT: Frozen tiramisu.

MAKES 4 servings

Nonstick cooking spray

1 **pound prepared meatloaf mixture**

1 **28-ounce jar spaghetti sauce**

ONE Preheat oven to 375°F. Coat a baking sheet with cooking spray; set aside.

TWO Form meatloaf mixture into 12 meatballs and place on prepared baking sheet. Bake 15 minutes or until internal temperature registers 155°F on an instant-read thermometer.

THREE Meanwhile, heat spaghetti sauce in saucepan; add meatballs.

PLAN AHEAD: Prepare recipe through Step Two. Cover and refrigerate up to 2 days. Reheat according to Step Three.

FREEZE AHEAD: Prepare recipe through Step Two. Cover and freeze up to 1 month. Defrost completely in refrigerator. Continue according to Step Three.

Quick and Light Beef and Noodles

KIDS LOVE THIS DISH!

SIDES: Sautéed Broccolini with Lemon and Feta (page 155) and Deb's Bread (page 125).

DESSERT: Root beer floats.

MAKES 6 servings

Nonstick cooking spray

2 **pounds ground beef**

½ **cup chopped onion**

1 **8-ounce package dried fine egg noodles, cooked according to package directions**

1 **cup light sour cream**

1 **10¾-ounce can reduced-fat and reduced-sodium condensed cream of mushroom soup**

1 **10¾-ounce can reduced-fat and reduced-sodium condensed cream of chicken soup**

1¾ **cups frozen corn**

1 **cup reduced-fat shredded cheddar cheese**

ONE Preheat oven to 375°F. Coat a 13x9x2-inch baking dish with cooking spray; set aside.

TWO In a large skillet cook ground beef and onion until meat is brown and onion is tender. Drain off fat. Stir in cooked pasta, sour cream, soups, frozen corn, and cheddar cheese. Transfer to prepared dish.

THREE Bake 25 minutes or until mixture is bubbly.

PLAN AHEAD: Prepare recipe through Step Two but don't preheat oven. Cover and refrigerate up to 2 days. Preheat oven. Continue according to Step Three.

FREEZE AHEAD: Prepare recipe through Step Two but don't preheat oven. Cover and freeze up to 1 month. Defrost completely in refrigerator. Preheat oven. Continue according to Step Three.

Perfectly Grilled Hamburgers

A SPECIAL FRIEND OF MINE RAISED NINE CHILDREN ON A LIMITED BUDGET BUT WITH UNLIMITED SPECIAL EFFECTS! HER KIDS KNEW THEY COULD INVITE FRIENDS OVER ON FRIDAY NIGHTS BECAUSE DAD COOKED HAMBURGERS ON THE GRILL AND THERE WERE ALWAYS EXTRAS. AS THEY GREW UP, THE CHILDREN INVITED THEIR DATES OVER FOR HAMBURGERS BEFORE GOING OUT FOR THE EVENING. YOU MIGHT WANT TO START A "FRIDAY-NIGHT SPECIAL" AT YOUR HOUSE!

SIDES: Parmesan Tomatoes (page 164) and Feta Cheese Potato Salad (page 139).

DESSERT: Hot fudge sundaes.

MAKES 4 servings

- 1½ to 2 pounds ground beef
- 1 cup ketchup
- ½ cup mayonnaise
- ¼ cup drained pickle relish
- 1 to 3 tablespoons grated onion
- Hamburger buns
- Lettuce leaves (optional)
- Thinly sliced onion (optional)
- Sliced pickles (optional)
- Sliced fresh mushrooms (optional)
- Sliced tomatoes (optional)
- Sliced American or cheddar cheese or blue cheese crumbles (optional)

ONE Lightly shape ground beef into four ¾-inch-thick patties.

TWO For a charcoal grill, grill patties on the rack of an uncovered grill directly over medium coals for 14 to 18 minutes or until done (160°F), turning once halfway through grilling. (For a gas grill, preheat grill. Reduce heat to medium. Place patties on grill rack over heat. Cover; grill as above.)

THREE Meanwhile, for sauce, in a bowl stir together ketchup, mayonnaise, pickle relish, and grated onion. Cover and refrigerate until serving time.

FOUR Remove burgers from grill. Serve burgers in buns. If desired, top with sauce, lettuce, onion, pickles, mushrooms, tomatoes, and/or cheese.

PLAN AHEAD: Prepare recipe through Step One. Cover and refrigerate up to 1 day. Continue according to Step Two.

FREEZE AHEAD: Prepare recipe through Step One. Cover and freeze up to 1 month. Defrost completely in refrigerator. Continue according to Step Two.

Mexican Beef with Corn Dumplings

FOR A SPECIAL MEMORY, SERVE THIS WARM, COMFORTING DINNER IN FRONT OF THE FIREPLACE OR AROUND THE COFFEE TABLE IN THE FAMILY ROOM.

SIDES: Tabbouleh (page 129) and Cran-Raspberry Molded Salad (page 136).

DESSERT: Frozen Banana Split Pie (page 189).

MAKES 4 servings

- 1 **pound ground beef**
- 1 **1¼-ounce envelope taco seasoning mix**
- ½ **cup chopped onion**
- 1 **14½-ounce can diced tomatoes, drained**
- 2 **cups frozen corn, thawed**
- 1 **4-ounce can chopped green chiles, drained**
- ½ **cup sliced, pitted black olives**
- 1 **10-ounce package corn bread mix**

ONE In a large skillet cook the ground beef until meat is brown. Drain off fat. Stir in taco mix, onion, drained tomatoes, corn, drained chiles, and olives. Cook and stir for 2 minutes.

TWO Prepare the corn bread according to package directions except use only half of the milk called for. Drop the batter by spoonfuls on top of the meat mixture. Cover and simmer 15 minutes.

PLAN AHEAD: Prepare recipe through Step One. Cover and refrigerate up to 1 day. Reheat over medium heat. Continue according to Step Two.

FREEZE AHEAD: Prepare recipe through Step One. Cover and freeze up to 1 month. Defrost completely in refrigerator. Reheat over medium heat. Continue according to Step Two.

Chili Soup

I SERVED THIS SOUP SEVERAL TIMES AT PARTIES FOR MY TEENAGERS. KEEP THE POT OF CHILI WARM ON THE STOVE TO MAKE IT EASY FOR THEM TO COME BACK FOR SECONDS.

BEEF

SIDES: Stovetop Corn Bread (page 117) and Apricot Salad (page 140).

DESSERT: Apple pie with vanilla ice cream.

MAKES 6 to 8 servings

- 1 **pound ground beef or turkey**
- 1 **cup chopped onion**
- 1 **1¼-ounce envelope taco seasoning mix**
- 1 **1-ounce envelope ranch dressing mix**
- 1 **15¼-ounce can whole kernel corn with Mexican seasoning, drained**
- 1 **15-ounce can Mexican-style pinto beans, rinsed and drained**
- 1 **15-ounce can chopped Mexican-style tomatoes, undrained**
- 1 **4-ounce can chopped green chiles, undrained**
- 1 **cup water**
  Shredded cheddar cheese

ONE In a 4-quart Dutch oven cook ground beef until meat is brown. Drain off fat.

TWO Stir in onion, taco seasoning, ranch dressing mix, drained corn, drained beans, undrained tomatoes, undrained chiles, and water. Simmer 15 to 20 minutes.

THREE Top individual servings with cheddar cheese.

PLAN AHEAD: Prepare recipe through Step Two. Cover and refrigerate up to 1 day. Reheat over low heat. Continue according to Step Three.

FREEZE AHEAD: Prepare recipe through Step Two. Cover and freeze up to 1 month. Defrost completely in refrigerator. Reheat over low heat. Continue according to Step Three.

Beef in Red Wine

THIS FANCY DISH IS DEFINITELY COMPANY-WORTHY. ANY LEFTOVERS ARE JUST AS DELICIOUS REHEATED THE NEXT DAY.

SIDES: Pesto Bow Ties (page 132) and Sautéed Spinach and Pine Nuts (page 157).

DESSERT: Apricot Nectar Cake with Lemon Glaze (page 184).

MAKES 6 servings

- 3 ounces bacon, slivered
- 1 medium onion, sliced
- 1 teaspoon minced fresh garlic
- 2 pounds beef round steak or sirloin steak, cut into 1-inch cubes
- ¼ cup flour
- 1 teaspoon salt
- ¼ teaspoon black pepper
- 3 cups red wine (such as Burgundy) or beef broth
- 1 teaspoon dried thyme, crushed
- 2 bay leaves
- 1 15-ounce package frozen pearl onions, thawed
- 1 pound fresh mushrooms, quartered

ONE In a Dutch oven cook bacon 3 to 5 minutes or until meat begins to brown. Stir in sliced onion and garlic; cook and stir 2 minutes or until onion is tender. Transfer mixture to a bowl; set aside.

TWO In the same Dutch oven brown half of the beef; remove beef from pan. Add remaining beef. Cook and stir until beef is brown. Return all beef and bacon mixture to Dutch oven.

THREE Sprinkle the flour, salt, and pepper over the meat and bacon mixture. Cook and stir over medium heat for 1 minute. Stir in wine, thyme, and bay leaves. Bring to boiling; reduce heat to low. Simmer, covered, 2 to 2½ hours or until meat is tender.

FOUR Stir pearl onions and mushrooms into mixture in Dutch oven; simmer, covered, another 20 minutes. Remove bay leaves before serving.

PLAN AHEAD: Prepare recipe through Step Three. Cover and refrigerate up to 2 days. Reheat over low heat. Continue according to Step Four.

FREEZE AHEAD: Prepare beef through Step Four. Cover and freeze up to 1 month. Defrost completely in refrigerator. Reheat over low heat.

Beef Stroganoff

THIS DISH IS ELEGANT ENOUGH FOR COMPANY YET SO EASY YOU WILL WANT TO MAKE IT AGAIN AND AGAIN FOR YOUR FAMILY.

SIDES: Sautéed Broccolini with Lemon and Feta (page 155) and crusty bread.

DESSERT: Pound cake topped with ice cream and chocolate sauce.

MAKES 6 servings

- 1½ **pounds sirloin or round steak**
- 1 **pound fresh mushrooms, sliced**
- 1 **cup chopped onion**
- 2 **tablespoons vegetable oil**
- 2 **cups beef broth**
- 2 **teaspoons paprika**
- 1 **teaspoon salt**
- ½ **teaspoon black pepper**
- 2 **cups sour cream**
- 2 **tablespoons flour**
- **Hot cooked rice or pasta**

ONE If desired, partially freeze beef for easier slicing. Trim fat from meat. Thinly slice meat across the grain into 2- to 3-inch strips.

TWO In a large skillet cook and stir the meat, mushrooms, and onion in hot oil over medium-high heat about 5 minutes. Drain off fat.

THREE Stir beef broth, paprika, salt, and pepper into mixture in skillet. Reduce heat and simmer, covered, 30 to 45 minutes or until beef is tender.

FOUR In a small bowl combine sour cream and flour. Stir into meat mixture in skillet. Cook and stir until sauce is thickened and bubbly (do not boil). Serve over rice.

PLAN AHEAD: Prepare recipe through Step Three. Cover and refrigerate up to 2 days. Continue according to Step Four.

FREEZE AHEAD: Prepare recipe through Step Three. Cover and freeze up to 1 month. Defrost completely in refrigerator. Continue according to Step Four.

OPTION: Chicken Stroganoff is also a great family dish. Substitute chicken strips for the beef and chicken broth for the beef broth. In Step Three simmer 20 minutes.

Skewered Steak Kabobs

KIDS LOVE EATING KABOBS BECAUSE THEY MAKE A REGULAR DINNER SEEM LIKE A PARTY.

BEEF

SIDES: Field Greens with Oranges and Ginger Dressing (page 149) and Grilled Onions with Balsamic Glaze (page 165).

DESSERT: Angel food cake topped with ice cream and fresh berries.

MAKES 4 to 6 servings

- 2 **pounds sirloin steak**
- ¾ **cup soy sauce**
- 2 **tablespoons toasted sesame oil**
- 1 **tablespoon grated fresh ginger**
- 1 **teaspoon minced fresh garlic**
- 4 **12-inch metal or wooden* skewers**

  Hot cooked rice tossed with sliced green onions (optional)

ONE Trim fat from meat. Cut into 1½-inch pieces. Place in a resealable bag set in a shallow bowl.

TWO In a bowl combine soy sauce, sesame oil, ginger, and garlic. Pour over meat. Seal bag. Marinate overnight in the refrigerator, turning occasionally.

THREE Thread meat onto skewers leaving ½-inch space between pieces. Grill kabobs on a grill rack directly over medium heat for 15 minutes, turning several times. (For a gas grill, preheat grill. Reduce heat to medium. Place kabobs on a grill rack over heat. Cover and grill as above.) Transfer to a serving platter. Cover and let sit 10 minutes before serving**. If desired, serve kabobs over hot cooked rice and green onions.

FREEZE AHEAD: Prepare recipe through Step Two. Freeze up to 1 month. Defrost completely in refrigerator. Continue according to Step Three.

*If using wooden skewers, soak them in water for at least 20 minutes before grilling. This will keep them from catching on fire.

**Letting cooked meat sit, or rest, a few minutes before serving allows the juices to redistribute, assuring juicy meat.

OPTION: To make Skewered Chicken Kabobs, use chicken breasts instead of steak and then follow the same recipe.

Seared Steak with Balsamic-Mushroom Glaze

MAKE THIS WHEN YOU CRAVE THE TASTE OF STEAK AND DON'T HAVE TIME TO LIGHT THE GRILL. BALSAMIC VINEGAR GIVES THE PERFECT TANG TO THE MILD MUSHROOMS. FOR EXTRA FLAVOR, TOP STEAK AND SAUCE WITH BLUE CHEESE CRUMBLES.

SIDES: Arizona Potatoes (page 166) and Baked Beans with Caramelized Onions and Orange Marmalade (page 169).

DESSERT: Black Forest Trifle (page 175).

MAKES 4 servings

- 1 **pound top round or sirloin steak, sliced thin (about ½-inch thick)***
- 1 **teaspoon salt**
- 1 **teaspoon black pepper**
- 2 **tablespoons olive oil**
- ⅓ **cup balsamic vinegar**
- 1 **6-ounce jar sliced mushrooms, drained (reserve 2 to 4 tablespoons of the liquid)**

ONE Toss sliced steak with salt and pepper; set aside. Heat olive oil in a large skillet over medium-high heat. Add steak to the skillet, making sure the pieces don't touch (you may have to do this in two batches). Quickly sear both sides of steak, being careful not to overcook. Transfer the meat to a plate.

TWO Add the vinegar and reserved mushroom juice to the skillet. Bring to boiling; boil until reduced by half, about 2 minutes. Remove pan from heat. Add the mushrooms, meat, and any accumulated juices from the plate; toss to coat.

PLAN AHEAD: Prepare recipe through Step Two. Cover and refrigerate up to 2 days. Reheat over medium-low heat.

FREEZE AHEAD: Prepare recipe through Step Two. Cover and freeze up to 1 month. Defrost completely in refrigerator. Reheat over medium-low heat.

* To make slicing easier, place steak in the freezer for 20 minutes. Partially frozen steak slices more easily.

Hearty Beef and Barley Stew

BARLEY IS A NUTRITIOUS, NUTTY-TASTING GRAIN WITH A FUN, CHEWY TEXTURE. ITS STARCHINESS GIVES DEPTH AND HEARTINESS TO THIS SOUP.

SIDES: Texas Toast (page 120) and Sautéed Spinach and Pine Nuts (page 157).

DESSERT: Chocolate cake with fudge frosting.

MAKES 6 to 8 servings

- 1½ pounds beef round steak
- 1 teaspoon salt
- ½ teaspoon black pepper
- 2 tablespoons plus 1 teaspoon canola oil
- ½ cup chopped onion
- ½ cup chopped carrot
- ½ cup chopped celery
- 6 cups beef broth
- ½ teaspoon dried thyme, crushed
- 1 cup pearl barley, rinsed
- 1 14½-ounce can diced tomatoes, undrained

ONE Cut steak into bite-size pieces; sprinkle with salt and pepper. In a large skillet brown meat on all sides in 2 tablespoons of the hot oil; remove from skillet. Add the remaining oil, the onion, carrot, and celery to the skillet. Cook and stir until vegetables are tender. Return the meat to the pan; stir in the beef broth. Bring to boiling; reduce heat to a simmer. Simmer, covered, 1½ hours.

TWO Stir in the thyme, barley, and undrained tomatoes. Continue to simmer the soup, covered, for 45 minutes more. Season to taste with salt and pepper.

PLAN AHEAD: Prepare soup through Step Two. Cover and refrigerate up to 2 days. Reheat over low heat.

FREEZE AHEAD: Prepare soup through Step Two. Cover and freeze up to 1 month. Defrost completely in refrigerator. Reheat over low heat.

Grilled Tuscan Steak with Warm Bean and Mushroom Compote

THIS SIMPLE STEAK RECIPE IS THE PRIDE AND JOY OF TUSCANY. THE WARM BEAN AND MUSHROOM COMPOTE COULD BE AN ENTRÉE ON ITS OWN. TOGETHER THEY ARE HEAVEN.

SIDE: Panzanella (page 142).

DESSERT: Baked Fruit (page 176).

MAKES 8 servings

- 3 to 4 pounds bone-in beef steak, such as Porterhouse or T-bone, cut 1 to 1½ inches thick
- 6 cloves garlic, slivered
- ¼ cup olive oil
- 2 tablespoons chopped fresh rosemary
- 2 tablespoons chopped fresh sage
- 3 teaspoons minced fresh garlic
- 1 teaspoon black pepper
  Salt to taste
- 1 recipe Warm Bean and Mushroom Compote

ONE Use a small paring knife to make slits in the steak; push slivers of garlic into the slits. Place steak in a resealable plastic bag set in a shallow bowl.

TWO For marinade, in a small bowl combine oil, rosemary, sage, minced garlic, pepper, and salt. Pour marinade over steak; seal bag. Marinate in the refrigerator 16 hours.

THREE Drain steak; discard marinade. For a charcoal grill, grill steak on the rack of an uncovered grill directly over medium coals for 12 to 15 minutes for medium-rare doneness (145°F), turning once halfway through grilling. (For a gas grill, preheat grill. Reduce heat to medium. Place steak on grill rack over heat. Cover and grill as above.)

FOUR To serve, cut into ½-inch slices. Serve with Warm Bean and Mushroom Compote.

WARM BEAN AND MUSHROOM COMPOTE: Brush 8 ounces fresh whole mushrooms with olive oil and season with salt and pepper. Grill mushrooms until soft, about 5 minutes per side. Cut mushrooms into ¼-inch slices. Place in a large bowl and stir in 2 cups drained, warmed white beans; 2 tablespoons chopped fresh parsley; 2 tablespoons chopped fresh thyme; 2 tablespoons chopped fresh rosemary; 2 tablespoons chopped fresh chives; 2 chopped roma tomatoes; ¼ cup fresh lemon juice; 3 tablespoons olive oil; 2 teaspoons minced fresh garlic; and ¼ cup grated Parmesan cheese.

FREEZE AHEAD: Prepare recipe through Step Two but do not marinate in refrigerator. Cover and freeze meat in marinade up to 1 month. Defrost completely in refrigerator. Continue according to Step Three.

Chris's Peanut Butter Stew

CHRIS MWAKA TAUGHT US HOW TO MAKE THIS FABULOUS, TASTY AFRICAN DISH. HIS MOM MADE IT OFTEN BACK HOME IN THE CONGO.

SIDES: Rice and tossed green salad.

DESSERT: Fresh fruit.

MAKES 6 servings

- 2 to 2½ pounds roast beef, braised until tender, cooking liquid reserved
- ½ cup chopped onion
- 1 clove garlic, chopped
- 2 tablespoons vegetable oil
- 1 6-ounce can tomato paste
- 1½ cups smooth peanut butter
- 1 quart liquid (cooking liquid plus water)
- 4 fresh mint leaves
  Salt and black pepper to taste
  Hot cooked rice or noodles or mashed potatoes

ONE Cut cooked meat into bite-size pieces and set aside. In Dutch oven or large saucepan sauté onion and garlic in hot oil until onion is tender and loses its raw aroma. Add tomato paste; cook and stir 1 minute. Stir in meat.

TWO Meanwhile, in a medium bowl whisk together the peanut butter and 1 cup of the reserved cooking liquid. When smooth, add another cup of liquid. Add the peanut butter mixture to the meat mixture and stir until smooth. Add more cooking liquid as needed to make a gravy consistency. Stir in mint. Taste and add salt and pepper as desired.

THREE Cook over low heat for 45 minutes, stirring often to keep from sticking. Serve stew over rice, noodles, or mashed potatoes.

OPTIONS: Cooked chicken or pork loin can be substituted for the roast beef.

Judie's Favorite Pot Roast Dinner

THIS IS AN ESSENTIAL DISH FOR YOUR RECIPE REPERTOIRE. THERE'S NOTHING EASIER THAN THROWING A ROAST IN A POT AND COOKING IT FOR A COUPLE OF HOURS. MY SECRET INGREDIENT, COFFEE, ADDS COLOR AND A DEEP, RICH FLAVOR, THOUGH NOT A COFFEE FLAVOR. NO ONE WILL GUESS YOU ADDED COFFEE BUT EVERYONE WILL RAVE ABOUT YOUR POT ROAST.

SIDES: Torn romaine with Caesar salad dressing and Angel Biscuits (page 208).

DESSERT: Mint Chocolate Sundaes: Top scoops of mint ice cream with chocolate sauce and a dollop of whipped cream.

MAKES 6 servings

- 1 2- to 2½-pound beef pot roast*
- 2 tablespoons vegetable oil
- 1 cup brewed coffee or beef broth

  Water to cover meat
- 1 teaspoon salt (or to taste)
- 1 teaspoon black pepper
- 2 bay leaves
- 3 or 4 large russet potatoes, peeled and cut into quarters
- 3 large onions, peeled and cut into quarters
- 3 large carrots, peeled and cut into large chunks
- ⅓ cup water
- ¼ cup flour

ONE Trim fat from meat. In a 4- to 6-quart Dutch oven brown meat on all sides in hot oil. Drain off fat. Stir in the coffee, enough water to cover the meat, the salt, pepper, and bay leaves. Bring to boiling; reduce heat. Simmer, covered, for 2 to 2½ hours or until the meat falls apart when you pierce it with a fork.

TWO Add potatoes, onions, and carrots and simmer, covered, another 40 minutes or until vegetables are tender. Transfer meat and vegetables to a serving platter, reserving juices. Discard bay leaves. Cover meat and vegetables with foil to keep warm.

THREE For gravy, return 2 cups of the reserved juices to the pan. Stir the ⅓ cup water into the flour. Stir into juices in pan. Cook and stir over medium heat until thickened and bubbly. Cook and stir for 1 minute more. Serve with meat and vegetables.

PLAN AHEAD: Prepare recipe through Step Two. Slice meat. Cover and refrigerate meat, vegetables, and reserved juices up to 1 day. Reheat over low heat. Continue according to Step Three.

FREEZE AHEAD: Prepare recipe through Step Two. Slice meat. Cover and freeze meat, vegetables, and reserved juices up to 1 month. Defrost completely in refrigerator. Reheat over low heat. Continue according to Step Three.

* Choose a rump, chuck, or tri-tip roast, or ask your butcher what is available that would work well for pot roast.

Vegetable Beef

THIS DINNER COOKS WHILE YOU WORK AROUND THE HOUSE. WHEN DINNERTIME COMES, SUPPER'S READY.

SIDES: Caesar Spinach Salad (page 146) and Texas Toast (page 120).

DESSERT: Ice Cream Snowballs: Roll scoops of ice cream in shredded coconut and freeze until firm. Serve on a puddle of chocolate sauce.

MAKES 4 to 6 servings

- 1 **pound beef stew meat**
- 2 **to 3 cups water or beef broth**
- 1 **cup chopped onion**
- ¾ **cup chopped green and/or red bell pepper**
- 1 **teaspoon minced fresh garlic**
- 1 **28-ounce can diced tomatoes, undrained**
- 1 **10-ounce package frozen mixed vegetables**
- ½ **cup uncooked white rice**
- 1 **teaspoon salt**
- ½ **teaspoon black pepper**

ONE Cover meat with water in a 4- to 6-quart Dutch oven. Cover Dutch oven and cook over medium heat for 1 hour. Add onion, bell pepper, and garlic. Cover and cook another hour.

TWO Stir in undrained tomatoes, mixed vegetables, rice, salt, and black pepper. Cover and cook 30 minutes or until rice is tender.

PLAN AHEAD: Prepare recipe through Step Two. Cover and refrigerate up to 3 days. Reheat over medium-low heat.

FREEZE AHEAD: Prepare recipe through Step Two. Cover and freeze up to 1 month. Defrost completely in refrigerator. Reheat over medium-low heat.

pork

Citrus Ginger Pork Loin

THIS PRETTY DISH IS ELEGANT ENOUGH FOR COMPANY. LEFTOVERS TASTE GREAT IN SANDWICHES.

SIDES: Mashed Sweet Potatoes (page 162) and Sautéed Asian Vegetables (page 159).

DESSERT: Caramel Sauce (page 194) drizzled over vanilla ice cream.

MAKES 6 servings

Nonstick cooking spray

1	3-pound boneless pork loin
1	teaspoon salt
½	teaspoon black pepper
2	tablespoons snipped fresh rosemary
1	tablespoon minced fresh garlic
1	tablespoon minced fresh ginger
1	cup white wine or chicken broth
1	cup orange marmalade

ONE Preheat oven to 350°F. Coat a 13x9x2-inch baking dish with cooking spray. Place pork loin in dish.

TWO In a small bowl combine salt, pepper, rosemary, garlic, and ginger. Spread mixture evenly over the meat. Pour wine into dish.

THREE Bake for 1 hour. Remove the pan from the oven.

FOUR Place marmalade in a small bowl; add 3 tablespoons of the meat drippings; mix well. Pour marmalade mixture over the roast. Return roast to the oven. Roast 30 minutes more or until desired doneness (145°F to 155°F), basting occasionally. Let stand 15 minutes. If desired, drizzle with pan juices.

PLAN AHEAD: Prepare recipe through Step Two but don't preheat oven. Cover and refrigerate up to 1 day. Preheat oven. Continue according to Step Three.

FREEZE AHEAD: Prepare recipe through Step Two but don't preheat oven. Cover and freeze up to 1 month. Defrost completely in refrigerator. Preheat oven. Continue according to Step Three.

Five-Spice Pork Loin

CHINESE FIVE-SPICE POWDER IS A ZESTY BLEND OF CLOVES, FENNEL SEED, STAR ANISE, CINNAMON, AND SZECHWAN PEPPER. THESE MILDLY EXOTIC FLAVORS COMBINE WITH PUNGENT SOY AND HOISIN SAUCES, BOLD GARLIC, SWEET HONEY, AND FRAGRANT ORANGE ZEST TO CREATE A FIVE-STAR DISH.

SIDES: Asparagus Salad (page 206) and Baked Beans with Caramelized Onions and Orange Marmalade (page 169).

DESSERT: Lemon Cream Cake: Slice a prepared pound cake horizontally into three layers. Spread half a can of lemon pie filling between layers. Frost the cake with whipped dessert topping. Garnish with lemon slices and fresh mint.

MAKES 8 servings

- 1 3- to 4-pound boneless pork loin
- 10 cloves garlic, each cut into 3 slices
- 2 teaspoons salt
- 1 teaspoon black pepper
- 3 tablespoons soy sauce
- 3 tablespoons sherry
- 3 tablespoons hoisin sauce
- 3 tablespoons honey
- 2 tablespoons orange zest
- 2 tablespoons Chinese five-spice powder

ONE Preheat oven to 425°F. Use a paring knife to make small slits in the pork loin. Push 1 slice of garlic into each slit. Place pork in a large roasting pan. Sprinkle meat with salt and pepper.

TWO In a medium bowl stir together soy sauce, sherry, hoisin sauce, honey, orange zest, and five-spice powder. Spread mixture onto meat.

THREE Bake 15 minutes. Reduce the oven temperature to 325°F. Bake another 45 to 60 minutes or to desired doneness (145°F to 155°F), basting with pan juices every 15 minutes.

FOUR Let stand for 10 minutes before slicing. If desired, drizzle with pan juices.

PLAN AHEAD: Prepare recipe through Step Two but don't preheat oven. Cover and refrigerate up to 1 day. Preheat oven. Continue according to Step Three.

FREEZE AHEAD: Prepare recipe through Step Two but don't preheat oven. Cover and freeze up to 1 month. Defrost completely in refrigerator. Preheat oven. Continue according to Step Three.

Baked BBQ Spareribs

I'VE INCLUDED THIS RECIPE BECAUSE PREP TIME IS SO SHORT AND THE RESULTS ARE INCREDIBLE. IT ALSO MAKES GREAT LEFTOVERS.

SIDES: Chantilly Fruit Salad (page 137) and Maui Wild Rice Pilaf (page 131).

DESSERT: Black Forest Pudding: Top prepared chocolate pudding with cherry pie filling and whipped dessert topping.

MAKES 4 servings

- 3 to 3½ pounds pork spareribs
- 1 cup pineapple juice
- 1 cup ketchup
- ½ cup thinly sliced green onions
- ¼ cup soy sauce
- 2 tablespoons packed brown sugar
- 2 tablespoons cider vinegar
- 2 tablespoons minced fresh ginger
- 2 teaspoons minced fresh garlic

ONE Preheat oven to 275°F. Cut ribs into serving-size pieces. Place ribs in an oven-proof 4- to 6-quart Dutch oven. Bake, covered, for 2 hours.

TWO Meanwhile, in a large bowl stir together pineapple juice, ketchup, green onions, soy sauce, brown sugar, vinegar, ginger, and garlic. Pour over the ribs.

THREE Bake, covered, for 1 hour more, turning the ribs after 30 minutes.

FOUR Transfer to a serving platter; drizzle with pan juices.

PLAN AHEAD: Prepare recipe through Step Two; cool ribs. Cover and refrigerate up to 1 day. Preheat oven. Continue according to Step Three.

FREEZE AHEAD: Prepare recipe through Step Two; cool ribs. Cover and freeze up to 1 month. Defrost completely in refrigerator. Preheat oven. Continue according to Step Three.

Bacon and Cheese Breakfast Pizzas

THESE ARE GREAT FOR A CROWD. USE BIG BAKING SHEETS TO COOK LOTS IN A HURRY.

SIDES: Arizona Potatoes (page 166) and Curried Melon Salad (page 141).

DESSERT: Vanilla yogurt topped with cherry pie filling.

MAKES 4 servings

4 slices bread

¼ cup mayonnaise

8 slices cooked bacon, crumbled

1 large tomato, thinly sliced

1 cup shredded cheddar cheese

Salt and black pepper to taste

ONE Preheat broiler. Place bread on a large baking sheet. Spread each slice with 1 tablespoon mayonnaise. Top each with crumbled bacon and tomato slices. Sprinkle with cheese, salt, and pepper.

TWO Broil 4 inches from the heat until bubbly.

PLAN AHEAD: Cook and crumble bacon. Cover and refrigerate up to 1 day.

Bacon and Cheddar Quiche

CHEESE LOVERS, THIS IS FOR YOU!

SIDES: Chantilly Fruit Salad (page 137) and Apricot-Walnut Scones (page 119).

DESSERT: Lemon Curd Swirls: Layer softened vanilla ice cream and purchased lemon curd in parfait glasses. Top with whipped dessert topping.

MAKES one 9-inch quiche

- 4 **large eggs**
- ½ **cup milk**
- 2 **tablespoons Dijon mustard**
- 5 **slices cooked bacon, crumbled**
- 2½ **cups shredded cheddar cheese**
- 1 **9-inch unbaked piecrust**

ONE Preheat oven to 350°F. In a large bowl whisk together eggs, milk, and mustard. Stir in crumbled bacon and cheese.

TWO Pour mixture into piecrust. Bake 40 minutes or until a knife inserted near the center comes out clean. If necessary, cover edge of crust with foil to prevent overbrowning. Let stand 10 minutes before serving.

PLAN AHEAD: Prepare recipe through Step One but don't preheat oven. Cover and refrigerate up to 1 day. Preheat oven. Continue according to Step Two.

FREEZE AHEAD: Prepare quiche. Cover and freeze up to 1 month. Defrost completely in refrigerator. Reheat in a 350°F oven 20 to 25 minutes or until hot.

Pasta with Kielbasa, Peppers, and Onions

SERVE THIS COMFORT DISH IN LARGE SOUP BOWLS. EAT WITH A SPOON TO GET EVERY LAST DROP OF THE FLAVORFUL SAUCE.

SIDES: Garlic Pita Crisps (page 126) and Cherry Tomato Salad (page 202).

DESSERT: Pudding Parfaits: Layer chocolate and vanilla pudding in parfait glasses.

MAKES 4 to 6 servings

- 1 **pound light kielbasa sausage, cut into ¼-inch slices**
- 1 **tablespoon olive oil**
- 1 **large onion, sliced**
- 1 **medium green bell pepper, sliced**
- 2 **to 3 teaspoons minced fresh garlic**
- 1 **cup white wine or chicken broth**

  Salt and black pepper to taste
- 1 **12-ounce package dried fettuccine, cooked according to package directions**

ONE In a large skillet cook and stir kielbasa in hot oil over medium-high heat 5 minutes or until light brown. Add onion, bell pepper, and garlic; cook and stir 5 minutes or until vegetables are tender. Add wine, salt, and black pepper; cook and stir 5 minutes more. Add pasta; toss to coat.

PLAN AHEAD: Prepare recipe. Cover and refrigerate up to 1 day. Reheat over low heat.

FREEZE AHEAD: Prepare recipe. Cover and freeze up to 1 month. Defrost completely in refrigerator. Reheat over low heat.

Sausage-Stuffed Tomatoes

THESE ARE AS PRETTY AS THEY ARE DELICIOUS. YOU'LL BE PROUD TO SERVE THEM TO COMPANY OR FOR A SPECIAL FAMILY MEAL.

SIDES: Deb's Bread (page 125) and Lemon and Feta Orzo Salad (page 134).

DESSERT: Sliced bananas and/or strawberries with hot fudge topping.

MAKES 6 servings

- 6 **medium ripe tomatoes**
- 1 **pound bulk sweet or hot Italian sausage**
- 1 **cup chopped onion**
- 3 **teaspoons minced fresh garlic**
- 2 **tablespoons balsamic vinegar**
- 1 **cup cooked white rice**
- 3 **tablespoons chopped fresh basil or 1 teaspoon dried basil, crushed**
- 3 **tablespoons chopped fresh parsley or 1 teaspoon dried parsley, crushed**
- 1 **large egg, lightly beaten**
- ½ **cup shredded mozzarella cheese**
- ½ **cup grated Parmesan cheese**
- 1 **teaspoon salt**
- 1 **teaspoon black pepper**

ONE Preheat oven to 375°F.

TWO Cut a thin slice from the top of each tomato. Scoop out and reserve pulp, leaving ¼-inch-thick shells; set aside. Chop pulp; set aside.

THREE In a large skillet cook sausage, onion, and garlic over medium heat until sausage is brown; drain off fat. Stir in reserved tomato pulp and vinegar. Simmer 5 minutes. Stir in cooked rice, basil, parsley, and egg. Stir in half of the mozzarella and half of the Parmesan cheese.

FOUR Place tomatoes in a 2-quart baking dish. Sprinkle the inside of tomatoes with salt and pepper. Spoon sausage mixture evenly into tomatoes, mounding on top. Sprinkle tomatoes with remaining cheese.

FIVE Bake 20 minutes or until heated through. Serve warm or at room temperature.

PLAN AHEAD: Prepare recipe through Step Five. Cover and let stand at room temperature up to 1 hour.

FREEZE AHEAD: Prepare recipe through Step Three but don't preheat oven or prepare tomatoes. Cover and freeze up to 1 month. Defrost completely in refrigerator. Preheat oven. Prepare tomatoes according to Step Two. Continue according to Step Four.

Smoked Ham and Fruit

PURCHASE SMOKED HAM SLICES, AVAILABLE IN MOST GROCERY STORES, OR USE LEFTOVERS FROM A BAKED HAM. THE MUSTARD SAUCE MELTS OVER THE HAM, FLAVORING THE PINEAPPLE AND BELL PEPPERS—DIVINE.

SIDES: Croissant Stuffing (page 124) and Cheesy Corn Casserole (page 167).

DESSERT: Best-Ever Pumpkin Pie (page 192).

MAKES 6 to 8 servings

Nonstick cooking spray

1   20-ounce can pineapple chunks, drained

1   15½-ounce can apricot halves, drained

2½ cups chopped onions

2   cups chopped green bell peppers

6   slices smoked ham (2 pounds total)

¼   cup brown mustard

¼   cup packed brown sugar

¼   cup apricot preserves

ONE Preheat oven to 375°F. Coat a 13x9x2-inch baking dish with cooking spray; set aside.

TWO Place drained pineapple chunks, drained apricot halves, onions, and bell peppers in prepared baking dish. Place ham slices on top of mixture.

THREE In a small bowl combine mustard, brown sugar, and apricot preserves. Spread on ham slices.

FOUR Bake, covered, for 20 minutes. Uncover and bake 5 to 10 minutes more.

PLAN AHEAD: Prepare recipe through Step Three but don't preheat oven. Cover and refrigerate up to 2 days. Preheat oven. Continue according to Step Four.

FREEZE AHEAD: Prepare recipe through Step Three but don't preheat oven. Cover and freeze up to 2 months. Defrost completely in refrigerator. Preheat oven. Continue according to Step Four.

OPTION: Substitute canned peaches, drained, for the pineapple chunks.

Skillet Frittata with Ham and Cheese

A SKILLET FRITTATA IS SIMILAR TO A LARGE OMELET THAT YOU DON'T HAVE TO TURN IN THE PAN. THIS ONE IS HEARTY AND PERFECT FOR A FAMILY MEAL OR CASUAL COMPANY SUPPER AT THE KITCHEN TABLE.

PORK

SIDES: Cran-Raspberry Molded Salad (page 136) and Strawberry Bread (page 122).

DESSERT: Baked Fruit (page 176).

MAKES 4 servings

- 5 large eggs
- 1 teaspoon salt
- ½ teaspoon black pepper
- ½ cup diced ham
- ½ cup chopped onion
- 1 tablespoon vegetable oil
- 1 cup finely shredded cheddar cheese

  Fresh flat-leaf parsley sprigs (optional)

ONE In a medium bowl whisk the eggs, salt, and pepper; set aside.

TWO In a large skillet cook and stir the ham and onion in hot oil over high heat until they begin to brown. Reduce heat to medium-low.

THREE Pour the egg mixture over ham mixture in skillet. As mixture sets, run a spatula around edge of skillet, lifting egg mixture so uncooked portion flows underneath. Continue cooking and lifting edges until egg mixture is set. Sprinkle with cheese. If desired, garnish with parsley.

PLAN AHEAD: Prepare recipe through Step One. Cover and refrigerate up to 1 day. Continue according to Step Two.

Ham and Red-Eye Sauce

COWBOYS USED TO FRY MEAT IN A SKILLET AND THEN POUR ON LEFTOVER COFFEE TO DEGLAZE THE PAN. LITTLE DID THEY KNOW THEY WERE INVENTING A CLASSIC DISH.

SIDES: Asparagus Salad (page 206) and Refrigerator Bran Muffins (page 116).

DESSERT: Frosted Chocolate Cookies (page 219) and ice cream.

MAKES 4 servings

- 4 slices cooked ham
- 1 tablespoon vegetable oil
- 1½ cups brewed coffee or one 14½-ounce can beef broth
- Salt and black pepper to taste

ONE In a large skillet brown the ham in hot oil over high heat, turning once. Transfer the ham to a serving platter.

TWO Add coffee to skillet and boil, scraping the bottom of the pan. Simmer 2 to 3 minutes or until liquid is slightly reduced. Season to taste with salt and pepper; serve sauce over ham.

FREEZE AHEAD: Prepare recipe through Step Two. Cover and freeze up to 1 month. Defrost completely in refrigerator. Reheat over low heat.

Pasta with Ham, Artichokes, and Feta

HAM AND PASTA MAKE THIS A KID-FRIENDLY MEAL. SERVE CHILLED FOR A DELICIOUS PASTA SALAD.

PORK

SIDES: Julie's Green Salad (page 147) and Parmesan Toasts (page 121).

DESSERT: Cheesecake served with sliced fresh strawberries.

MAKES 4 servings

- 1 **6-ounce jar marinated artichokes, undrained**
- 1 **cup chopped cooked ham**
- ½ **cup sliced green onions**
- 1 **pound dried pasta, cooked according to package directions (reserve ½ cup cooking water, if needed)**
- ½ **cup crumbled feta cheese**

  Salt and black pepper to taste

ONE Drain artichoke hearts, reserving the liquid. Coarsely chop artichoke hearts. Add artichoke hearts and reserved liquid to a large skillet over medium-high heat. Stir in ham, green onions, and cooked pasta. Cook, stirring occasionally, until heated through. (Add some of the reserved cooking water if mixture needs moisture.)

TWO Transfer to a serving platter. Sprinkle with the feta, salt, and pepper.

PLAN AHEAD: Prepare recipe through Step One. Cover and refrigerate up to 1 day. Reheat over low heat. Continue according to Step Two.

OPTIONS: Use chopped cooked chicken or Polish sausage instead of ham. Use Parmesan, cheddar, or Monterey Jack instead of feta cheese.

No-Work Meatballs and Spaghetti

THE CASINGS OF THE SAUSAGE SHRINK TO FORM LITTLE MEATBALLS AS THE SAUSAGE COOKS. TA-DA!

SIDES: Caesar Spinach Salad (page 146) and Parmesan Toasts (page 121).

DESSERT: Broiler S'Mores: Place graham crackers on a baking sheet. Top with pieces of chocolate and marshmallows. Broil until marshmallows melt. Top each with another graham cracker.

MAKES 4 to 6 servings

1   **pound Italian sausage in casings, cut into 1-inch pieces**

1   **26-ounce jar pasta sauce**

1   **pound dried angel hair pasta, cooked according to package directions**

1   **tablespoon olive oil**

ONE In a large saucepan combine sausage pieces and pasta sauce. Simmer, covered, for 20 minutes.

TWO Meanwhile, toss cooked pasta with olive oil. Serve sauce mixture over pasta.

PLAN AHEAD: Prepare recipe through Step One. Cover and refrigerate up to 2 days. Reheat over low heat. Continue according to Step Two.

FREEZE AHEAD: Prepare recipe through Step One. Cover and freeze up to 1 month. Defrost completely in refrigerator. Reheat over low heat. Continue according to Step Two.

OPTION: Extra Dinner—Meatball Pizza: Double the recipe ingredients for the meatballs. Refrigerate half of the meatballs for up to 2 days. Spread some of the sauce on a prepared pizza crust; top with meatballs. Bake according to pizza crust directions.

Smothered Pork Chops

MY MOM MADE THESE CHOPS FOR OUR BIG FAMILY OF FIVE KIDS. THE MEAT WOULD FALL OFF THE BONE. THIS MEAL IS A COZY CHILDHOOD MEMORY.

SIDES: Arizona Potatoes (page 166) and Tomatoes Stuffed with Creamed Spinach (page 161).

DESSERT: Coconut cream pie.

MAKES 4 servings

- 2 tablespoons vegetable oil
- ½ cup flour
- 1 teaspoon seasoned salt
- ½ teaspoon black pepper
- 4 pork loin chops, cut 1 to 1¼ inches thick
- 1 medium onion, cut into ½-inch slices
- 2 teaspoons minced fresh garlic
- Water

ONE In a large skillet preheat the oil over medium-high heat.

TWO Meanwhile, in a shallow bowl combine flour, seasoned salt, and pepper. Coat both sides of each chop with flour mixture.

THREE Brown both sides of chops in hot oil. Top chops with onion and garlic. Pour enough water in the skillet to cover chops. Simmer, covered, 20 to 30 minutes or until pork is tender (160°F).

FREEZE AHEAD: Prepare recipe. Cover and freeze up to 1 month. Defrost completely in refrigerator. Reheat over low heat.

Mexican Pork Chops and Rice

MILD GREEN CHILES AND CHILI POWDER ADD A SOUTHWESTERN EDGE TO THIS RECIPE.

SIDE: Cheesy Corn Casserole (page 167).

DESSERT: Cinnamon ice cream and sugar cookies.

MAKES 6 servings

- 2 **tablespoons vegetable oil**
- 6 **boneless pork top loin chops, cut 1 inch thick**
- ½ **cup uncooked white rice**
- 1 **large onion, sliced**
- 1 **medium green bell pepper, sliced**
- 1 **4-ounce can diced green chiles, undrained**
- 1 **28-ounce can diced tomatoes, undrained**
- 2 **teaspoons chili powder**
- 1 **teaspoon ground cumin**
- 1 **teaspoon salt**
- 1 **cup water**

ONE Preheat oil in an extra-large skillet over medium-high heat. Cook pork chops in hot oil about 14 minutes or until done (160°F), turning once. Add remaining ingredients in the following order: rice, onion, bell pepper, undrained chiles, undrained tomatoes, chili powder, cumin, salt, and water.

TWO Cook, covered, over medium-low heat 45 minutes or until rice is tender.

PLAN AHEAD: Prepare recipe through Step One. Cover and refrigerate up to 2 days. Continue according to Step Two.

Stuffed Pork Chops

APPLE, ONION, AND SAGE ADD INCREDIBLE AROMA AND
TASTE TO THESE CHOPS.

SIDES: Chop Chop Salad (page 201) and Cheddar Rice (page 130).

DESSERT: Purchased cream puffs filled with chocolate pudding.

MAKES 6 servings

Nonstick cooking spray

6 pork loin chops, cut 1¼ inches thick

1½ cups finely chopped onions

½ cup chopped celery

¼ cup butter

⅔ cup finely chopped cooking apple

2 tablespoons chopped fresh parsley

1 teaspoon rubbed sage

1 teaspoon dried thyme, crushed

½ teaspoon salt

¼ teaspoon black pepper

3 cups soft white bread crumbs

1 large egg, lightly beaten

1 cup chicken broth

1 cup apple juice

ONE Preheat oven to 375°F. Coat a 13x9x2-inch baking dish with cooking spray; set aside.

TWO Make a pocket in each chop by cutting horizontally from the fat side almost to the bone; set aside.

THREE In a large skillet cook onions and celery in hot butter over medium-high heat 10 minutes or until vegetables are tender. Stir in apple, parsley, sage, thyme, salt, and pepper. Cook and stir 5 minutes. Remove from heat and stir in bread crumbs, egg, and broth; toss to combine. Divide filling evenly among chops, saving any extra to spoon around chops in baking dish.

FOUR Place chops and any extra stuffing in prepared baking dish. Pour apple juice over chops. Bake, covered, 25 minutes. Uncover and bake another 20 minutes or until chops are done (160°F).

PLAN AHEAD: Prepare recipe through Step Three but do not preheat oven or coat dish. Cover and refrigerate up to 1 day. Preheat oven. Coat dish. Continue according to Step Four.

FREEZE AHEAD: Prepare recipe through Step Three but do not preheat oven or coat dish. Cover and freeze up to 2 months. Defrost completely in refrigerator. Preheat oven. Coat dish. Continue according to Step Four.

poultry

POULTRY

Chicken Pot Pie

USE THE TASTY FILLING, THINNED WITH A LITTLE MILK, TO MAKE CHICKEN À LA KING. SERVE OVER HOT COOKED NOODLES.

SIDE: Chantilly Fruit Salad (page 137).

DESSERT: Crazy Chocolate Cake (page 185).

MAKES 4 to 6 servings

- 1 15-ounce package rolled refrigerator unbaked piecrust (2 crusts)
- 1 purchased whole large roasted chicken
- 1 cup frozen chopped onions and bell peppers, thawed
- ½ cup frozen loose-pack peas, thawed
- 1 2-ounce jar chopped pimiento, drained
- ½ teaspoon black pepper
- 1 15-ounce jar Alfredo sauce
- 1 egg mixed with 1 tablespoon water, to make an egg glaze

ONE Preheat oven to 375°F. Let piecrusts stand according to package directions. Remove meat from chicken and cut into bite-size pieces. Discard skin and bones. You should have about 4 cups meat.

TWO In a large bowl combine chicken, onions and bell peppers, peas, drained pimiento, black pepper, and Alfredo sauce.

THREE Unroll piecrust. Line a 9-inch pie pan with 1 piecrust. Fill with chicken mixture. Top with second piecrust; crimp edges and brush with egg glaze.

FOUR Bake 25 to 35 minutes or until crust is golden brown.

PLAN AHEAD: Prepare recipe through Step Two except do not preheat oven or prepare piecrusts. Cover and refrigerate up to 1 day. Preheat oven and let piecrusts stand according to package directions. Continue according to Step Three.

FREEZE AHEAD: Prepare recipe though Step Three. Cover and freeze up to 1 month. Defrost completely in oven. Continue according to Step Four.

Chicken Spaghetti Casserole

I MADE THIS DOZENS OF TIMES WHEN RAISING MY KIDS. IT MAKES A LOT SO IT IS GREAT FOR A CROWD.

SIDES: Caesar Spinach Salad (page 146) and Deb's Bread (page 125).

DESSERT: Million Dollar Cream Pie (page 191).

MAKES 10 servings

- 1 purchased whole roasted chicken
- 1½ cups chopped onions
- 1½ cups chopped celery
- 1½ cups chopped green bell pepper
- ½ cup butter
- 3 14-ounce cans chicken broth
- 3 cups tomato juice
- ½ cup sliced pimiento-stuffed green olives
- 3 tablespoons chili powder
- 2 teaspoons salt
- 1 pound dried spaghetti, cooked according to package directions
- 1 pound processed American cheese, cut into cubes

ONE Remove meat from chicken, cutting into bite-size pieces; discard skin and bones. (You should have about 3 cups meat.) Set chicken aside.

TWO In a large skillet cook and stir onions, celery, and bell pepper in hot butter over medium heat for 15 minutes or until vegetables are tender. Stir in chicken, chicken broth, tomato juice, olives, chili powder, and salt. Simmer, uncovered, 30 minutes; stir occasionally.

THREE Meanwhile, preheat oven to 350°F. Stir cooked pasta into sauce; toss to coat. Stir in cheese. Place mixture in a 13x9x2-inch baking dish (if mixture won't all fit, place the remaining in a 9x9x2-inch baking dish). Bake 30 minutes or until bubbly.

PLAN AHEAD: Prepare recipe through Step Two. Cover and refrigerate up to 2 days. Continue according to Step Three.

FREEZE AHEAD: Prepare through Step Two. Cover and freeze up to 1 month. Defrost completely in refrigerator. Continue according to Step Three.

Cream of Chicken Soup

TO SIMPLIFY, USE FROZEN CHOPPED ONION-AND-CELERY BLEND (SOME BRANDS ALSO INCLUDE BELL PEPPERS) AND CARROTS. A ROASTED CHICKEN FROM THE DELI IS PERFECT IN THIS SOUP.

SIDES: Texas Toast (page 120) and Curried Melon Salad (page 141).

DESSERT: Cherry Meringue Cloud (page 172).

MAKES 6 servings

- 1 **purchased whole roasted chicken**
- 1½ **cups chopped carrots**
- 1 **cup chopped celery**
- ½ **cup chopped onion**
- ½ **cup butter**
- ½ **cup plus 1 tablespoon flour**
- 7 **cups low-sodium chicken broth**
- 3 **tablespoons chopped fresh parsley**
- ½ **teaspoon dried thyme, crushed**
- 1 **bay leaf**
- ½ **cup whipping cream**
- 2½ **teaspoons dry sherry (optional)**
   Salt and black pepper

ONE Remove meat from chicken, cutting into bite-size pieces; discard skin and bones. (You should have about 3 cups meat.) Set chicken aside.

TWO In a 4- to 6-quart Dutch oven cook and stir carrots, celery, and onion in hot butter over medium heat for 15 minutes or until vegetables are tender. Sprinkle the flour over the vegetable mixture; cook and stir 2 minutes. Slowly add the chicken broth to the pan and bring to boiling, stirring constantly. Add parsley, thyme, and bay leaf to the pot. Reduce heat to medium-low; simmer, uncovered, 15 minutes. Add the chicken; bring to boiling.

THREE Stir in the whipping cream and, if desired, sherry. Season to taste with salt and pepper. Remove bay leaf before serving.

PLAN AHEAD: Prepare recipe through Step Three. Cover and refrigerate up to 2 days. Reheat over low heat .

FREEZE AHEAD: Prepare recipe through Step Three. Cover and freeze up to 1 month. Defrost completely in the refrigerator. Reheat over low heat.

Chicken and Green Chile Stew

MILD GREEN CHILES ADD A BRIGHT TONE TO ENSURE THIS ISN'T JUST AN EVERYDAY STEW. COOKING A WHOLE CHICKEN IS AN EASY TASK BUT IF YOU WANT TO SAVE THIS STEP, USE A COOKED DELI CHICKEN AND A CAN OF CHICKEN BROTH IN PLACE OF THE RESERVED LIQUID.

SIDES: Tortillas, shredded lettuce, chips, and salsa.

DESSERT: Caramel-Banana Sundaes: Top vanilla ice cream with sliced bananas. Sprinkle with cinnamon and drizzle with caramel topping.

MAKES 6 servings

- 1 3- to 3½-pound chicken or 2 whole chicken breasts
- 1 cup coarsely chopped onion
- 1 cup chopped green bell pepper
- 2 teaspoons minced fresh garlic
- 1 tablespoon cooking oil
- 1 4-ounce can chopped green chiles, undrained
- 1 14½-ounce can diced tomatoes, undrained
- 4 medium potatoes, peeled and cubed
- 1 cup chopped carrot
- 1 teaspoon salt (or to taste)
- 1 teaspoon black pepper (or to taste)

ONE Place chicken in a Dutch oven; add enough water to cover chicken. Simmer, covered, 30 to 45 minutes or until meat is falling off the bone. Remove chicken from the pan. When cool, shred the chicken meat; set aside. Reserve the cooking liquid.

TWO In a large saucepan cook and stir onion, bell pepper, and garlic in hot oil over medium-high heat for 5 minutes. Add the chicken, undrained chiles, undrained tomatoes, potatoes, and carrots; simmer, covered, 20 minutes. Stir in enough reserved cooking liquid to reach desired consistency. Add salt and black pepper.

PLAN AHEAD: Prepare recipe through Step Two. Cover and refrigerate up to 1 day. Reheat over low heat.

FREEZE AHEAD: Prepare recipe through Step Two. Cover and freeze up to 1 month. Defrost completely in refrigerator. Reheat over low heat.

Asian Chicken Wraps

CHOOSE YOUR FAVORITE INGREDIENTS IN ANY AMOUNT AND IN ANY COMBINATION. THAT'S WHAT MAKES THIS SUPPER SO MUCH FUN.

POULTRY

SIDE: Apricot Salad (page 140).

DESSERT: Instant Banana Pudding (page 174).

MAKES 8 to 10 wraps

Finely chopped fresh vegetables, such as bell peppers, cucumbers, and/or tomatoes

Cooked rice and/or beans

Chopped cooked chicken, ham, turkey, and/or hard-cooked eggs

Shredded cheese

1   **head iceberg lettuce**

Assorted dipping sauces or salad dressings

ONE Spoon ¼ cup of desired ingredients onto lettuce leaves. Fold bottom edge of each lettuce leaf up and over filling. Fold in opposite sides; roll up from bottom. Serve with desired dipping sauces.

PLAN AHEAD: Wash lettuce, prepare vegetables, chop meat, and cook rice. Cover and refrigerate up to 1 day.

Chicken Piccata

EVERYONE LOVES THIS ELEGANT AND EASY DISH. SPRAYING THE CHICKEN WITH NONSTICK COOKING SPRAY BEFORE POUNDING PREVENTS TEARING.

POULTRY

SIDES: Buttered noodles, Asparagus Salad (page 206), and Sautéed Zucchini with Walnuts (page 160).

DESSERT: Frozen Banana Split Pie (page 189).

MAKES 4 servings

- 4 **medium boneless, skinless chicken breast halves (1½ pounds total)**
- **Nonstick cooking spray**
- 1 **cup all-purpose flour**
- ½ **teaspoon salt**
- ½ **teaspoon black pepper**
- ½ **teaspoon paprika**
- 2 **tablespoons olive oil**
- ¼ **cup butter**
- 10 **cloves garlic, chopped**
- ½ **cup finely chopped onion**
- ½ **cup freshly squeezed lemon juice**
- 1 **cup white wine**
- ½ **cup capers**
- ¼ **cup chopped fresh parsley**
- **Salt and black pepper to taste**

ONE Coat chicken breasts with nonstick cooking spray. Place each chicken breast half between two pieces of plastic wrap. Using flat side of a meat mallet, pound chicken lightly to about ¼ inch thick. Remove plastic wrap.

TWO In a shallow dish stir together flour, salt, pepper, and paprika. Dip the chicken in the flour mixture to coat both sides.

THREE In a large skillet cook chicken in hot oil over medium heat for 2 to 3 minutes per side or until golden. Transfer chicken to a serving platter.

FOUR Add butter, garlic, and onion to the skillet. Cook and stir until onion is tender. Add lemon juice and white wine to skillet, stirring to loosen brown bits in bottom of skillet. Bring to boiling. Boil gently, uncovered, for 5 to 8 minutes or until liquid is reduced by about half. Stir in capers and parsley. Season to taste with salt and pepper. Spoon sauce over chicken.

PLAN AHEAD: Prepare recipe through Step One. Cover and refrigerate up to 1 day. Continue according to Step Two.

FREEZE AHEAD: Prepare recipe through Step One. Cover and freeze up to 1 month. Defrost completely in refrigerator. Continue according to Step Two.

Basil Grilled Chicken Breasts

EVERYONE LOVES TO GRILL CHICKEN. THE BIG TRICK IS TO KEEP IT MOIST AND JUICY. HERE IS THE SOLUTION.

SIDES: Lemon and Feta Orzo Salad (page 134) and Sautéed Red Cabbage (page 156).

DESSERT: Apple Dumplings with Cinnamon Sauce (page 179).

MAKES 4 servings

- 4 **medium boneless, skinless chicken breast halves (1½ pounds total)**
- 2 **tablespoons olive oil**
- ½ **cup snipped fresh basil**
- 2 **tablespoons fresh lemon juice**
- **Salt and black pepper to taste**

ONE Place chicken in a resealable plastic bag set in a shallow dish. For marinade, in a bowl combine olive oil, basil, lemon juice, salt, and pepper. Pour marinade over chicken; seal bag. Marinate in the refrigerator for 1 to 2 hours, turning once. Drain chicken, reserving marinade*.

TWO For a charcoal grill, grill chicken on the rack of an uncovered grill directly over medium coals for 12 to 15 minutes or until chicken is no longer pink (170°F), turning halfway through grilling. (For a gas grill, preheat grill. Reduce heat to medium. Place chicken on grill rack over heat. Cover and grill as above.) Brush with reserved marinade during the last 5 minutes of grilling.

MARINADE VARIATIONS

SOY SAUCE WITH LIME MARINADE: Prepare as above except use 2 tablespoons soy sauce, 1 teaspoon black pepper, and 2 tablespoons fresh lime juice; omit olive oil, basil, lemon juice, and salt.

GINGER CILANTRO MARINADE: Prepare as above except use 1 tablespoon olive oil, 2 tablespoons fresh lime juice, 1 teaspoon minced fresh garlic, 3 tablespoons minced fresh cilantro, 1 tablespoon minced fresh ginger, 1 teaspoon salt, and 1 teaspoon black pepper; omit basil, lemon juice, and salt and black pepper.

OLIVE OIL AND LEMON MARINADE: Prepare as above except omit basil.

PLAN AHEAD: Prepare recipe through Step One. Refrigerate up to 1 day. Continue according to Step Two.

FREEZE AHEAD: Prepare recipe through Step One. Freeze up to 1 month. Defrost completely in refrigerator. Continue according to Step Two.

*NOTE: Marinades may be used on chicken after cooking if they are first boiled for 2 minutes to kill any bacteria from the raw chicken.

Chicken and Rolled Dumplings

MY GRANDMOTHER ALWAYS MADE HER DUMPLINGS FROM A DOUGH SIMILAR TO THAT USED FOR PIECRUST. TO SAVE TIME, USE PREPARED PIECRUST DOUGH. YOUR HOUSE WILL SMELL DIVINE WHEN YOU COOK THIS CHICKEN RECIPE.

SIDE: Cherry Tomato Salad (page 202).

DESSERT: Quick Fruit Crisp (page 177).

MAKES 6 servings

- **3** boneless, skinless chicken breast halves (about 1¼ pounds total)
- **6** cups water
- **2** cubes chicken bouillon
- **2** teaspoons salt
- **1** teaspoon Italian seasoning
- **2** bay leaves
- **1** cup frozen peas and carrots
- **½** of a 15-ounce package rolled refrigerated unbaked pie crust (1 piecrust), cut into strips
- **½** cup flour

ONE Slice each chicken breast into 6 or 8 pieces. Place in a large saucepan; cover with water. Bring to a simmer over high heat; skim any foam off the top. Reduce heat to medium-low. Stir in bouillon cubes, salt, Italian seasoning, and bay leaves. Use a wooden spoon to break chicken into bite-size pieces. Add frozen peas and carrots; bring to boiling.

TWO Meanwhile, dip each pastry strip into flour, coating both sides. Place pastry strips, one at a time, on boiling mixture. Do not stir. Simmer 10 minutes or until pastry strips are cooked through.

PLAN AHEAD: Prepare recipe through Step One. Cover and refrigerate up to 2 days. Reheat over low heat. Continue according to Step Two.

FREEZE AHEAD: Prepare recipe through Step One. Cover and freeze up to 1 month. Defrost completely in refrigerator. Reheat over low heat. Continue according to Step Two.

Italian Chicken and Pasta

THE DISTINCT AND ROBUST FLAVORS OF SUN-DRIED TOMATOES, FRESH BASIL, AND KALAMATA OLIVES MAKE THIS DISH TASTE LIKE A CHEF HAS BEEN COOKING FOR YOU.

POULTRY

SIDES: Garlic toast and Asparagus Salad (page 206).

DESSERT: Raspberry Italian Ice (page 180).

MAKES 6 servings

- 2 tablespoons olive oil
- 1 pound skinless, boneless chicken breast halves, sliced into diagonal strips

  Salt and black pepper to taste

- ½ cup slivered oil-packed sun-dried tomatoes
- 1 tablespoon minced fresh garlic
- ¼ cup chopped fresh basil
- 1 13¾-ounce can artichoke hearts, drained
- ½ cup sliced, pitted kalamata olives
- ½ to 1 cup chicken broth
- 1 pound dried angel hair pasta, cooked according to package directions
- ¼ cup crumbled feta cheese

ONE In a large skillet heat olive oil over medium-high heat. Sprinkle chicken strips with salt and pepper. Cook and stir chicken strips in the hot oil 3 to 4 minutes or until light brown. Add tomatoes, garlic, basil, drained artichokes, olives, and chicken broth to skillet. Cook and stir 10 minutes or until chicken is no longer pink.

TWO Add cooked pasta to skillet; toss to coat. Transfer to a serving platter and top with feta.

PLAN AHEAD: Prepare recipe through Step One. Cover and refrigerate up to 2 days. Reheat over low heat. Continue according to Step Two.

FREEZE AHEAD: Prepare recipe through Step One. Cover and freeze up to 1 month. Defrost completely in refrigerator. Reheat over low heat and continue according to Step Two.

Chicken Breasts Stuffed with Goat Cheese

I HAVE MADE THESE FOR LARGE DINNER PARTIES. THEY CAN BE ASSEMBLED AHEAD AND BAKED JUST BEFORE SERVING.

SIDES: Parmesan Tomatoes (page 164) and Angel Biscuits (page 208).

DESSERT: Instant Berry Tarts: Fill purchased individual tart shells with vanilla pudding. Top with blueberries and sliced strawberries. Brush melted apple jelly over the fruit.

MAKES 4 servings

Nonstick cooking spray

3 ounces soft goat cheese

½ cup pitted kalamata olives, finely chopped

¼ cup slivered sun-dried tomatoes

1 tablespoon chopped fresh rosemary or 2 teaspoons dried rosemary, crushed

½ cup fine dry bread crumbs

½ cup shredded Parmesan cheese

4 medium chicken breast halves, skinned (about 4 pounds total)

Salt and black pepper to taste

1 cup dry white wine or chicken broth

ONE Preheat oven to 375°F. Coat a 13x9x2-inch baking dish with cooking spray; set aside.

TWO For filling, in a small bowl combine goat cheese, olives, tomatoes, and rosemary; set aside.

THREE For topping, in a small bowl combine bread crumbs and Parmesan cheese; set aside.

FOUR Make a pocket* in each chicken breast half. Sprinkle chicken with salt and pepper. Spoon filling into pockets. Place filled chicken breasts in prepared dish; pour wine into baking dish. Sprinkle chicken with topping.

FIVE Bake 30 to 45 minutes or until chicken is no longer pink (170°F).

PLAN AHEAD: Prepare recipe through Step Four but don't preheat oven. Cover and refrigerate up to 1 day. Preheat oven. Continue according to Step Five.

FREEZE AHEAD: Prepare chicken through Step Four but don't preheat oven. Cover and freeze up to 1 month. Defrost completely in the refrigerator. Preheat oven. Continue according to Step Five.

*****NOTE:** To make a pocket, place a chicken breast on a cutting board. Beginning in the center of one side, horizontally insert a thin, sharp knife about three-fourths of the way through the meat, moving the knife in a fanning motion to create a pocket. Repeat with remaining chicken pieces.

Crispy Chicken and Sausage

SAUSAGE AND PARMESAN CHEESE—THAT'S ALL YOU HAVE TO SAY ABOUT THIS RECIPE FOR CRISP, OVER-THE-TOP, TASTY CHICKEN. YOUR KIDS WILL LOVE THESE MORE THAN ANY DRIVE-THROUGH CHICKEN STRIPS.

SIDES: Pesto Bow Ties (page 132) and Sautéed Spinach and Pine Nuts (page 157).

DESSERT: Frozen Raspberry Cream Pie (page 190).

MAKES 4 servings

Nonstick cooking spray

4 ounces mild Italian sausage links

1 cup Rice Krispies® or Special K® cereal

¼ cup grated Parmesan cheese

1 teaspoon minced fresh garlic

1 teaspoon dried oregano, crushed

1 teaspoon dried basil, crushed

½ teaspoon salt

¼ teaspoon black pepper

1 large egg

4 medium boneless, skinless chicken breast halves (1½ pounds total), cut into thick strips

ONE Preheat oven to 350°F. Coat a baking sheet with cooking spray; set aside.

TWO Remove casings from sausage, if present. In a large skillet cook and stir sausage over medium-high heat until light brown. Remove from skillet; drain on paper towels.

THREE Crush cereal in a food processor or place in a resealable plastic bag and crush with a rolling pin.

FOUR In a large shallow bowl combine sausage, crushed cereal, cheese, garlic, oregano, basil, salt, and pepper. In a medium shallow bowl beat the egg until frothy.

FIVE Dip each piece of chicken in the egg, then roll in the cereal mixture, pressing the cereal onto chicken. Place chicken on prepared baking sheet making sure the pieces don't touch.

SIX Bake for 30 to 40 minutes or until chicken is no longer pink (170°F).

PLAN AHEAD: Prepare coating mixture. Cover and refrigerate up to 2 days.

FREEZE AHEAD: Prepare coating mixture. Cover and freeze up to 1 month. Defrost in the refrigerator.

Sweet-and Sour-Chicken

THERE ARE NUMEROUS RECIPES FOR SWEET-AND-SOUR SAUCES. THIS IS ONE OF THE SIMPLEST AND MOST DELICIOUS.

SIDE: Steamed rice.

DESSERT: Rainbow sherbet and shortbread cookies.

MAKES 6 servings

- 1 8-ounce can pineapple chunks, juice reserved and combined with water to make 1 cup
- 1 cup cider vinegar
- 1 cup chicken broth
- ¼ cup soy sauce
- 1¼ cups sugar
- 4 cups cubed cooked chicken breast
- 3 cups frozen Oriental stir-fry vegetables
- ¼ cup cornstarch

ONE In a Dutch oven combine pineapple chunks, reserved juice and water, vinegar, ½ cup of the broth, the soy sauce, and sugar. Bring to a simmer, stirring to dissolve the sugar. Add chicken and frozen vegetables to skillet; simmer, covered, 10 minutes.

TWO Whisk together the remaining ½ cup chicken broth and the cornstarch until smooth. Whisk into the chicken mixture; cook and stir until mixture thickens and turns clear.

PLAN AHEAD: Cook chicken up to 2 days ahead.

FREEZE AHEAD: Prepare recipe through Step One. Cover and freeze up to 1 month. Defrost completely in refrigerator. Reheat over low heat. Continue according to Step Two.

Bruschetta Chicken Bake

THE FLAVORS OF ITALIAN BRUSCHETTA MAKE THIS CHICKEN A FAVORITE AT SUPER SUPPERS.

SIDES: Green beans and Jacques Pepin's Cranberry Sauce (page 170).

DESSERT: Instant Tiramisu Cups: For each dessert, line a teacup with one ladyfinger cookie. Drizzle with a little coffee-flavored syrup and top with vanilla pudding. Dust top with ¼ teaspoon cinnamon.

MAKES 6 servings

Nonstick cooking spray

6   medium boneless, skinless chicken breast halves (2½ pounds total)

1   teaspoon dried basil, crushed

1   cup shredded mozzarella cheese

2½ cups Uncle Ben's® Classic Corn Bread Stuffing mix

1   14½-ounce can diced tomatoes, undrained

½   cup chicken broth

2   teaspoons minced fresh garlic

ONE Preheat oven to 400°F. Spray a 13x9x2-inch baking dish with cooking spray. Place chicken breasts in dish. Sprinkle evenly with basil and cheese.

TWO In a medium bowl combine stuffing mix, undrained tomatoes, broth, and garlic. Spoon over chicken in dish.

THREE Bake 30 to 40 minutes or until chicken is no longer pink (170°F).

PLAN AHEAD: Prepare recipe through Step Two but don't preheat oven. Cover and refrigerate up to 1 day. Preheat oven. Continue according to Step Three.

FREEZE AHEAD: Prepare recipe through Step Two but don't preheat oven. Cover and freeze up to 1 month. Defrost completely in refrigerator. Preheat oven. Continue according to Step Three.

Hunter's Chicken

THIS DISH CAN ALSO BE MADE WITH CHICKEN BREAST HALVES. USE ABOUT 2 POUNDS OF WHITE MEAT.

SIDE: Panzanella (page 142).

DESSERT: Chocolate Toffee Matzos (page 181).

MAKES 4 servings

- 1 3- to 3½-pound chicken, cut into 8 pieces
- ¼ cup olive oil or vegetable oil
- 2 28-ounce cans diced tomatoes, undrained
- ½ cup pitted black olives
- 3 teaspoons minced fresh garlic
- 2 tablespoons chopped fresh rosemary or 1 teaspoon dried rosemary, crushed
- 1 teaspoon salt (or to taste)
- ½ teaspoon black pepper (or to taste)
- 4 cups hot cooked rice or pasta

ONE In a large skillet cook chicken pieces in hot oil over medium heat for 15 minutes, turning once. Stir in undrained tomatoes, olives, garlic, rosemary, salt, and pepper. Simmer, covered, for 20 minutes or until chicken is no longer pink (170°F for breasts; 180°F for thighs and drumsticks).

TWO Serve chicken mixture over hot cooked rice.

PLAN AHEAD: Prepare recipe through Step One. Cover and refrigerate up to 1 day. Reheat mixture over low heat. Continue according to Step Two.

FREEZE AHEAD: Prepare recipe through Step One. Cover and freeze up to 1 month. Defrost completely in refrigerator. Reheat mixture over low heat. Continue according to Step Two.

Chicken, Rice, and Artichoke Casserole

I'VE BEEN MAKING THIS SINCE I WAS A NEWLYWED. I'VE SUCCESSFULLY USED ALL KINDS OF RICE: WHITE, BROWN, AND WILD RICE BLENDS. BROWN AND WILD RICE MAY TAKE LONGER TO COOK.

SIDES: Cherry Tomato Salad (page 202) and Parmesan Toasts (page 121).

DESSERT: Fresh or canned peach slices topped with whipped dessert topping and maraschino cherries.

MAKES 6 to 8 servings

Nonstick cooking spray

- 4 **cups water**
- 2 **cups uncooked long grain white rice**
- 1 **teaspoon salt**
- ½ **cup chopped onion**
- ½ **cup sliced celery**
- 1 **tablespoon butter or vegetable oil**
- 4 **medium boneless, skinless chicken breast halves (about 1½ pounds total)**
- 1 **10¾-ounce can reduced-fat cream of mushroom soup**
- ½ **cup milk, white wine, or chicken broth**
- 1 **6-ounce can sliced mushrooms, undrained**
- 1 **cup shredded cheddar cheese**
- 1 **13¾-ounce can quartered artichoke hearts, drained**

ONE Coat a 13x9x2-inch baking dish with cooking spray; set aside.

TWO In a large saucepan combine water, rice, and salt. Simmer, covered, over medium heat 15 minutes or until rice is tender. Transfer rice to prepared baking dish.

THREE Meanwhile, preheat oven to 375°F. In a large saucepan cook and stir the onion and celery in hot butter until tender. Stir in chicken, soup, milk, undrained mushrooms, cheese, and drained artichokes. Spread mixture over rice in prepared baking pan.

FOUR Bake 15 to 20 minutes or until bubbly.

PLAN AHEAD: Prepare recipe through Step Three but don't preheat oven. Cover and refrigerate up to 1 day. Preheat oven. Continue according to Step Four.

FREEZE AHEAD: Prepare recipe through Step Three but don't preheat oven. Cover and freeze up to 1 month. Defrost completely in refrigerator. Preheat oven. Continue according to Step Four.

Rosemary Roasted Chicken

THIS IS AN ALL-TIME FAVORITE AT OUR COOKING SCHOOL. NONCOOKS LOVE IT BECAUSE IT IS SO EASY YET LOOKS AND TASTES GOURMET—LIKE THE ONES FROM THE FRENCH CAFES!

SIDES: Tabbouleh (page 129) and Sautéed Broccolini with Lemon and Feta (page 155).

DESSERT: Raspberry Italian Ice (page 180).

MAKES 6 servings

- ¼ cup butter, softened
- 2 teaspoons seasoned salt
- 2 tablespoons chopped fresh garlic
- 2 tablespoons dried rosemary, crushed
- 1 4-pound roasting chicken
- 1 tablespoon vegetable oil

ONE In a small bowl combine butter, seasoned salt, garlic, and rosemary; set aside.

TWO Preheat oven to 375°F. Rinse inside of chicken; pat dry with paper towels. Starting at the breast bone, use your fingers to loosen the skin from the meat, leaving skin attached at the top. Spread butter mixture evenly under the skin. Skewer neck skin of chicken to the back; tie legs to tail. Twist wing tips under back.

THREE Place chicken, breast side up, on a rack in a shallow roasting pan. Brush chicken with vegetable oil and sprinkle with additional seasoned salt. If desired, insert a meat thermometer into the center of an inside thigh muscle (thermometer should not touch bone).

FOUR Roast, uncovered, for 1 to 1¼ hours or until drumsticks move easily in their sockets and chicken is no longer pink (180°F). Remove chicken from oven. Cover; let stand 10 minutes before carving.

PLAN AHEAD: Prepare recipe through Step Two but do not preheat oven. Cover and refrigerate up to 1 day. Preheat oven. Continue according to Step Three.

FREEZE AHEAD: Prepare recipe through Step Two but do not preheat oven. Cover and freeze up to 1 month. Defrost completely in refrigerator. Preheat oven. Continue according to Step Three.

Cornish Game Hens with Fruit and Nuts

THIS STUFFING IS A BEAUTIFUL AND DELICIOUS TWIST ON THE USUAL BREAD VARIETY. IT ALSO GOES WELL WITH ANY GRILLED MEAT.

SIDES: Cheesy Stuffed Potatoes (page 205) and Angel Biscuits (page 208).

DESSERT: Best-Ever Pumpkin Pie (page 192).

MAKES 4 servings

- 4   1-pound Cornish game hens
- 4 to 6 teaspoons minced fresh garlic
- 1   tablespoon dried thyme, crushed
- 1   tablespoon rubbed sage
- 1   teaspoon salt
- 1   teaspoon black pepper
- ½   cup red wine vinegar or apple juice
- ¼   cup olive oil
- ½   cup dried plums
- ½   cup dried apricots
- ½   cup pitted green olives
- ½   cup pecan pieces
- ¼   cup capers
- 4   bay leaves
- ½   cup packed brown sugar
- ½   cup chicken broth

ONE Rinse inside of hens; pat dry with paper towels. Place hens in a large bowl.

TWO In a medium bowl combine garlic, thyme, sage, salt, pepper, vinegar, olive oil, plums, apricots, olives, pecans, capers, and bay leaves. Pour over hens in bowl. Cover and marinate overnight in refrigerator.

THREE Preheat oven to 350°F. Place hens, breast sides up, on a rack in a shallow roasting pan. Twist wing tips under back. Spoon marinade over hens; sprinkle evenly with brown sugar. Pour chicken broth around hens in pan.

FOUR Bake 1 to 1½ hours or until an instant-read thermometer inserted into the thigh of each hen registers 180°F (thermometer should not touch bone) and juices run clear.

FIVE Arrange hens and stuffing on a serving platter. Drizzle with some of the pan juices.

PLAN AHEAD: Prepare hens through Step Two. Cover and refrigerate up to 1 day. Continue according to Step Three.

FREEZE AHEAD: Prepare hens through Step Two. Cover and freeze up to 1 month. Defrost completely in the refrigerator. Continue according to Step Three.

Teriyaki Chicken Wings

THESE ARE THE EASIEST WINGS IN THE WORLD TO MAKE, BUT ARE SO YUMMY YOU'LL BE LICKING YOUR FINGERS TO GET EVERY LAST DROP OF SAUCE.

SIDE: Corn and Water Chestnuts: Prepare frozen corn and add a can of sliced water chestnuts.

DESSERT: Fortune cookies with rainbow sherbet.

MAKES 4 servings

- 18 **meaty chicken wings (about 3 pounds)**
- 1 **tablespoon sesame oil**
- 1 **cup bottled teriyaki sauce**
- 1 **teaspoon dried red pepper flakes (optional)**

ONE Preheat oven to 375°F.

TWO Cut off and discard tips of chicken wings. Cut wings at joints to form 36 pieces. In a large bowl toss chicken wings with sesame oil.

THREE Place wings in a single layer on a baking sheet. Bake for 25 to 35 minutes or until chicken is tender and no long pink, turning once.

FOUR Toss wings with teriyaki sauce and, if desired, red pepper flakes.

PLAN AHEAD: Prepare recipe through Step Two but do not preheat oven. Place wings and sesame oil in plastic bag and refrigerate up to 1 day. Preheat oven. Continue according to Step Three.

FREEZE AHEAD: Prepare recipe through Step Two but do not preheat oven. Place wings and sesame oil in freezer bag and freeze up to 1 month. Thaw in refrigerator. Preheat oven. Continue according to Step Three.

seafood

Sesame Shrimp

NOWADAYS, IT'S EASY TO FIND FROZEN, PEELED TAIL-ON SHRIMP AT THE GROCERY STORE. THE SESAME-GARLIC MARINADE ADDS INCREDIBLE FLAVOR.

SEAFOOD

SIDES: Sautéed Asian Vegetables (page 159) and steamed rice.

DESSERT: Lemon Tarts: Fill individual baked tart shells with prepared lemon curd. Top with whipped dessert topping.

MAKES 4 servings

- ¼ cup toasted sesame oil
- 2 teaspoons minced fresh garlic
- 16 peeled and deveined uncooked jumbo* shrimp, tails left on
- 1½ cups flour
- 1 tablespoon baking powder
- 1 teaspoon salt
- 1½ cups beer or water
- ¼ cup sesame seeds
  Vegetable oil for frying

ONE In a large bowl combine sesame oil and garlic. Cut each shrimp lengthwise along the underside, being careful not to cut all the way through. Place split shrimp on a cutting board and flatten with the flat side of a metal spatula. Add flattened shrimp to sesame oil mixture; toss to coat. Cover and refrigerate 30 minutes or up to 8 hours.

TWO Meanwhile, for batter, in a large bowl combine flour, baking powder, and salt. Whisk in the beer until smooth. Stir in sesame seeds.

THREE In a large skillet heat vegetable oil over medium heat. Hold a shrimp by the tail and dip into the batter. Slip into the hot oil. Repeat with remaining shrimp. Cook, turning shrimp gently, 3 minutes or until golden brown. Use a slotted spoon to remove shrimp to paper towels to drain.

PLAN AHEAD: Prepare recipe through Step Two. Cover and refrigerate up to 8 hours. Continue according to Step Three.

* Jumbo shrimp are usually 21 to 25 pieces per pound.

Shrimp Alfredo

A JAR OF ALFREDO SAUCE MAKES THIS RECIPE EASY AND QUICK.

SIDES: Buttered green peas and Caesar Spinach Salad (page 146).

DESSERT: Baked Fruit (page 176).

MAKES 4 servings

- 1   15-ounce jar prepared Alfredo sauce
- 1½   pounds peeled and deveined uncooked large shrimp
- 1   12-ounce package dried linguini, cooked according to package directions
- 2   tablespoons Parmesan cheese (or to taste)

ONE In a large skillet combine Alfredo sauce and shrimp over medium heat. Cook and stir 3 to 4 minutes or until shrimp are opaque.

TWO Serve shrimp over pasta and sprinkle with Parmesan cheese.

PLAN AHEAD: Prepare recipe through Step One. Cover and refrigerate up to 1 day. Reheat over low heat. Continue according to Step Two.

FREEZE AHEAD: Prepare recipe through Step One. Cover and freeze up to 1 month. Defrost completely in refrigerator. Reheat over low heat. Continue according to Step Two.

OPTIONS: Stir in ¼ cup sun-dried tomatoes, 2 tablespoons minced fresh parsley, and/or ¼ cup pine nuts. This recipe can also be made with meat from a purchased whole roasted chicken instead of shrimp.

Thai Coconut-Peanut Shrimp on Rice

COCONUT IS A CLASSIC THAI INGREDIENT, PERFECT FOR SWEETENING HOT AND SPICY DISHES.

SEAFOOD

SIDE: Sautéed Asian Vegetables (page 159).

DESSERT: Orange sherbet.

MAKES 4 to 6 servings

- 1 **cup canned coconut milk**
- ½ **cup bottled Asian peanut sauce**
- 2 **pounds peeled and deveined uncooked shrimp**
- ½ **to 1 teaspoon Asian hot sauce (optional)**
- 4 **cups hot cooked white rice**
- ½ **cup coconut chips or shredded coconut**

Chopped peanuts (optional)

ONE In a large skillet combine coconut milk and peanut sauce; stir in shrimp. Cook and stir over medium heat 3 to 4 minutes or until shrimp are opaque. If desired, stir in hot sauce.

TWO Serve shrimp and sauce over hot cooked rice and sprinkle with coconut and, if desired, peanuts.

PLAN AHEAD: Prepare recipe through Step One. Cover and refrigerate up to 1 day. Reheat shrimp and sauce in a saucepan over medium heat. Continue according to Step Two.

FREEZE AHEAD: Prepare recipe through Step One. Cover and freeze up to 1 month. Defrost completely in refrigerator. Reheat shrimp and sauce in a saucepan over medium heat. Continue according to Step Two.

Shrimp Creole

THIS FULL-FLAVORED DISH IS A SNAP TO MAKE.

SIDES: Steamed rice and romaine lettuce topped with blue cheese crumbles, croutons, and oil-and-vinegar dressing.

DESSERT: Warm apple pie with vanilla ice cream.

MAKES 4 servings

- 1 12-ounce package frozen chopped onions and bell peppers, thawed
- 1 teaspoon minced fresh garlic
- 1 tablespoon vegetable oil
- 1 15-ounce can diced tomatoes, undrained
- 1 4-ounce jar chopped pimiento, drained
- 1 teaspoon salt (or to taste)
- ½ teaspoon black pepper (or to taste)
- 1 pound peeled and deveined uncooked shrimp

ONE In a large skillet cook and stir onions and bell peppers and garlic in hot oil 2 minutes over medium-high heat. Stir in undrained tomatoes, drained pimiento, salt, and black pepper. Bring to a simmer.

TWO Add shrimp to skillet. Cook and stir 2 to 3 minutes or until shrimp are opaque.

PLAN AHEAD: Prepare recipe. Cover and refrigerate up to 1 day. Reheat over low heat.

FREEZE AHEAD: Prepare recipe. Cover and freeze up to 1 month. Defrost completely in refrigerator. Reheat over low heat.

Shrimp with Mustard Sauce

YOU'LL FEEL LIKE A GOURMET CHEF WHEN YOU SERVE THIS, YET IT IS SIMPLE AND QUICK TO PREPARE. FROZEN SHRIMP IS A GREAT SHORTCUT.

SIDES: Steamed rice or buttered noodles and Field Greens with Oranges and Ginger Dressing (page 149).

DESSERT: Million Dollar Cream Pie (page 191).

MAKES 6 servings

- 2 **tablespoons olive oil**
- 36 **peeled and deveined uncooked medium shrimp**
- 4 **shallots, minced**
- 2 **tablespoons minced fresh tarragon or thyme**
- ¼ **cup dry sherry or chicken broth**
- ½ **cup whipping cream**
- 1 **cup butter, cut into pieces**
- 2 **tablespoons Dijon mustard**
- 1 **teaspoon salt (or to taste)**
- ½ **teaspoon black pepper (or to taste)**

ONE In a large skillet heat olive oil over medium heat. Add shrimp; cook and stir 3 to 4 minutes or until shrimp are opaque. Remove shrimp from skillet and keep warm in a covered bowl.

TWO For sauce, add shallots and tarragon to the skillet. Cook and stir for 2 minutes. Reduce heat to low. Add sherry and cream; simmer until sauce thickens and coats the back of a spoon. Stir in butter one piece at a time, stirring after each addition. Stir in mustard, salt, and pepper. Pour sauce over shrimp in bowl; toss gently to coat.

PLAN AHEAD: Prepare recipe. Cover and refrigerate up to 1 day. Reheat over low heat.

FREEZE AHEAD: Prepare recipe. Cover and freeze up to 1 month. Defrost completely in refrigerator. Reheat over low heat.

Seafood Linguini

SHALLOTS, ARTICHOKE HEARTS, SHRIMP, AND SCALLOPS COMBINE TO TELL YOU THIS IS A SPECIAL MEAL.

SIDES: Deb's Bread (page 125) and Julie's Green Salad (page 147).

DESSERT: Black Forest Trifle (page 175).

MAKES 4 to 6 servings

- 2 **shallots, minced (about ¼ cup)**
- 2 **teaspoons minced fresh garlic**
- 1 **tablespoon olive oil**
- 1 **16-ounce can artichoke hearts, drained and halved**
- 1 **cup chicken broth**
- 1½ **cups dry white wine or chicken broth**
- 1 **pound peeled and deveined uncooked shrimp**
- 1 **pound fresh sea scallops**
- 1 **teaspoon chopped fresh thyme or ½ teaspoon dried thyme, crushed**
- 2 **tablespoons fresh lemon juice**
- 1 **teaspoon salt**
- ½ **teaspoon black pepper**
- 1 **12-ounce package dried linguini, prepared according to package directions**

ONE In a large skillet cook and stir shallots and garlic in hot oil 2 minutes over medium heat. Stir in drained artichoke hearts, broth, and wine; simmer 2 minutes.

TWO Add shrimp and scallops to skillet and simmer 3 to 4 minutes or until shrimp and scallops are opaque. Remove seafood from pan using a slotted spoon and keep warm in a covered bowl.

THREE Bring sauce in pan to boiling; boil until reduced by half. Return seafood to pan. Stir in thyme, lemon juice, salt, and pepper. Cook and stir until heated through.

FOUR Serve over linguini.

PLAN AHEAD: Prepare recipe through Step Three. Cover and refrigerate up to 1 day. Reheat over medium heat. Continue according to Step Four.

FREEZE AHEAD: Prepare recipe through Step Three. Cover and freeze up to 1 month. Defrost completely in refrigerator. Reheat over low heat. Continue according to Step Four.

Shrimp and Goat Cheese Quesadillas with Avocado Salsa

TANGY GOAT CHEESE GIVES A KICK TO THE SHRIMP.

SIDE: Corn and Black Bean Salad with Chili-Lime Dressing (page 150).

DESSERT: Mango sorbet.

MAKES 2 servings

- 2 10-inch flour tortillas
- 12 to 14 peeled and deveined cooked medium shrimp
- ½ cup crumbled goat cheese
- 1 large tomato, chopped and drained
- 1 to 2 tablespoons sliced jalapeños (optional)
- ¼ cup chopped fresh cilantro
- ¼ cup chopped sweet onion
- 1 ripe avocado, peeled
- 2 tablespoons fresh lime juice
- 1 teaspoon salt (or to taste)

ONE Preheat a skillet over medium heat. Place 1 tortilla in skillet. Arrange shrimp evenly on the tortilla; sprinkle with goat cheese, drained tomatoes, jalapeños (if desired), and cilantro. Top with second tortilla and cook 3 minutes. Flip the quesadilla and cook 2 minutes more or until both sides are golden.

TWO Meanwhile, for avocado salsa, in a food processor combine onion, avocado, lime juice, and salt. Process until mixed well but still a bit chunky, stopping to scrape down sides as needed.

THREE Remove the quesadilla to a cutting board and cut into wedges. Serve with avocado salsa.

PLAN AHEAD: Prepare avocado salsa. Cover and refrigerate up to 4 hours.

OPTION: Substitute cooked chicken, sausage, or pinto or red beans for the shrimp.

Slow Cooker Jambalaya

THIS COLORFUL DISH WILL MAKE ANY MEAL A PARTY. ASSEMBLE BEFORE WORK SO WHEN YOU ARRIVE HOME, A FABULOUS DINNER IS ALMOST DONE.

SIDES: Steamed rice, Angel Biscuits (page 208), and Apricot Salad (page 140).

DESSERT: Instant Banana Pudding (page 174).

MAKES 12 servings

- 1 **pound skinless, boneless chicken breast halves, cut into 1-inch cubes**
- 1 **pound andouille sausage, cut into ½-inch slices**
- 1 **28-ounce can diced tomatoes, undrained**
- 1 **cup chopped onion**
- 1 **cup chopped green bell pepper**
- 1 **cup sliced celery**
- 1 **cup chicken broth**
- 1 **tablespoon minced fresh garlic**
- 1 **teaspoon dried oregano, crushed**
- 1 **teaspoon Cajun seasoning**
- ½ **teaspoon dried thyme, crushed**
- ½ **teaspoon cayenne pepper (or to taste)**
- 1 **pound peeled and deveined cooked shrimp**
- ¼ **cup minced fresh flat-leaf parsley**

ONE In a slow cooker combine chicken, sausage, undrained tomatoes, onion, bell pepper, celery, chicken broth, garlic, oregano, Cajun seasoning, thyme, and cayenne pepper.

TWO Cover and cook 7 to 8 hours on low-heat setting or 3 to 4 hours on high-heat setting. Stir in shrimp for the last 20 minutes of cooking. Just before serving, sprinkle with parsley.

PLAN AHEAD: Prepare recipe through Step One. Cover and refrigerate up to 1 day. Continue according to Step Two.

FREEZE AHEAD: Prepare recipe through Step One. Transfer to an airtight container. Freeze up to 1 month. Defrost completely in refrigerator. Place mixture in slow cooker. Continue according to Step Two.

Quick-and-Easy Crab and Noodle Soup

ONE CAN OF CRAB GOES A LONG WAY IN THIS DELICIOUS SOUP.

SEAFOOD

SIDES: Parmesan Toasts (page 121) and Asparagus Salad (page 206).

DESSERT: Apple Dumplings with Cinnamon Sauce (page 179).

MAKES 4 servings

- ½ cup chopped green onions
- 1 cup sliced celery
- ½ cup thinly sliced carrot
- 2 tablespoons butter
- 2 15-ounce cans chicken broth
- ¼ cup dry sherry (optional)
- 1 6-ounce can crabmeat, drained, flaked, and cartilage removed
- 3 ounces dried egg noodles, cooked according to package directions
- 2 tablespoons fresh lemon juice
- 1 teaspoon salt (or to taste)
- ½ teaspoon black pepper (or to taste)

  Chopped fresh parsley

ONE In a large saucepan cook and stir green onions, celery, and carrot in hot butter for 5 minutes or until vegetables are tender. Stir in chicken broth and, if desired, sherry; simmer 5 minutes. Stir in crab, cooked noodles, and lemon juice. Season to taste with salt and pepper; heat through.

TWO Ladle soup into bowls and garnish with parsley.

PLAN AHEAD: Prepare soup. Cover and refrigerate up to 1 day. Reheat over low heat. Continue according to Step Two.

FREEZE AHEAD: Prepare soup. Cover and freeze up to 1 month. Defrost in refrigerator. Reheat over low heat. Continue according to Step Two.

Poached Salmon with Green Mayonnaise

YOU WILL BE PROUD OF THIS BEAUTIFUL, FLAKY FISH. THE UNIQUE SAUCE IS DELICIOUS ON ANY FISH.

SIDES: Pearl Couscous Salad (page 199) and crusty bread.

DESSERT: Ice cream topped with sliced strawberries and grated dark chocolate.

MAKES 6 servings

- 1½ cups dry white wine or chicken broth
- 1½ cups water
- 1 lemon, sliced
- 1 small onion, sliced
- 1 bay leaf
- 1 2-pound salmon fillet
- 1 recipe Green Mayonnaise

ONE In a fish poacher or large skillet combine wine, water, lemon, onion, and bay leaf. Bring to boiling.

TWO Add salmon to poacher or skillet (if using a skillet, you may need to cut salmon into smaller pieces). Reduce heat to low. Simmer, covered, about 8 minutes or until fish is flaky.

THREE Carefully transfer salmon to serving platter. Serve with Green Mayonnaise.

GREEN MAYONNAISE: In a food processor combine 1 tablespoon lemon juice, 1 cup fresh parsley or spinach, 2 tablespoons snipped fresh tarragon, 2 tablespoons sliced green onion, 1 teaspoon minced fresh garlic, 2 tablespoons capers, and 1½ to 2 cups mayonnaise. Process until mixture is smooth, stopping to scrape down sides as needed.

PLAN AHEAD: Prepare Green Mayonnaise. Cover and refrigerate up to 2 days.

FREEZE AHEAD: Prepare salmon through Step Two. Cover and freeze up to 1 month. Defrost completely in refrigerator. Reheat under a preheated broiler. Continue according to Step Three.

Baked Salmon Fillets with Lemon-Dill Sauce

LOVELY SALMON FILLETS BAKE EASILY, AND THE DILL SAUCE MAKES A PERFECT COMPANION.

SIDES: Sautéed Broccolini with Lemon and Feta (page 155) and Lemon and Feta Orzo Salad (page 134).

DESSERT: Apricot Nectar Cake with Lemon Glaze (page 184).

MAKES 6 servings

Nonstick cooking spray

1   2-pound skinless salmon fillet

2   tablespoons olive oil or sesame oil

2   teaspoons salt

1   teaspoon black pepper

3   tablespoons fresh lemon juice

1   recipe Lemon-Dill Sauce

Lemon wedges (optional)

ONE Preheat oven to 475°F. Spray a baking sheet with cooking spray; set aside.

TWO Slice the salmon into ½-inch pieces and place in a single layer on prepared baking sheet. Brush each piece of fish with olive oil and sprinkle with salt, pepper, and lemon juice.

THREE Bake 10 minutes or until the fish is flaky. Serve with Lemon-Dill Sauce and, if desired, lemon wedges.

LEMON-DILL SAUCE: In a medium bowl stir together 1 cup sour cream, ½ cup mayonnaise, 3 tablespoons lemon juice, ¼ cup snipped fresh dill, and salt and pepper to taste.

PLAN AHEAD: Prepare recipe through Step Two but don't preheat oven. Cover and refrigerate up to 8 hours. Prepare Lemon-Dill Sauce. Cover and refrigerate up to 2 days. Preheat oven. Continue according to Step Three.

Skillet Fish Fillets with Lemon-Mustard Sauce

YOU'LL LOVE THIS EASY WAY TO COOK FISH, AND THE SIMPLE YET CLASSIC LEMON SAUCE MAKES IT ELEGANT.

SEAFOOD

SIDES: Sautéed Zucchini with Walnuts (page 160) and Field Greens with Oranges and Ginger Dressing (page 149).

DESSERT: Pound cake topped with ice cream and thawed frozen mixed berries.

MAKES 4 servings

- 8 **thin fish fillets (about 1 pound total), such as tilapia, grouper, or catfish**
- 1 **to 2 teaspoons seasoned salt**
- 2 **tablespoons olive oil or vegetable oil**
- 1 **tablespoon butter**
- ½ **cup fresh lemon juice**
- 1 **tablespoon Dijon mustard**
- 2 **tablespoons white wine or chicken broth**
- ½ **teaspoon salt (or to taste)**
- ½ **teaspoon black pepper (or to taste)**

ONE Sprinkle both sides of each fish fillet with seasoned salt.

TWO In a large skillet heat oil and butter. Add fish in a single layer; cook over medium-high heat 1 minute. Turn carefully; cook 1 to 2 minutes more or until fish is flaky. Transfer fish to a serving platter; cover with foil to keep warm.

THREE Add lemon juice, mustard, and wine to the skillet. Bring to a simmer. Cook and stir 3 to 4 minutes or until sauce is slightly reduced. Season to taste with salt and pepper. Serve fish with sauce.

PLAN AHEAD: Prepare recipe through Step One. Cover and refrigerate 8 hours. Continue according to Step Two.

Tuscan Tuna and Bean Bruschetta

THIS TRADITIONAL ITALIAN COMBINATION OF WHITE BEANS AND TUNA IS DELIGHTFUL ATOP CRUSTY BREAD.

SIDE: Cherry Tomato Salad (page 202).

DESSERT: Baked Fruit (page 176).

MAKES 4 servings

- 1 15-ounce can cannellini beans, rinsed and drained
- 1 12-ounce can tuna, drained and flaked
- 1 small red onion, thinly sliced
- 2 tablespoons drained capers
- 1 tablespoon minced fresh sage or 2 teaspoons dried sage, crushed
- ¼ cup fresh lemon juice
- 2 tablespoons red wine vinegar
- 2 tablespoons olive oil
- 1 teaspoon minced fresh garlic
- 1 teaspoon salt (or to taste)
- ½ teaspoon black pepper (or to taste)
- 1 baguette cut into ½-inch slices and toasted

ONE In a large bowl combine drained beans, tuna, onion, capers, and sage.

TWO For dressing, in a small bowl whisk together lemon juice, vinegar, olive oil, garlic, salt, and pepper. Drizzle dressing on bean mixture; toss to combine.

THREE Serve immediately with baguette slices.

PLAN AHEAD: Prepare recipe through Step One. Cover and refrigerate up to 1 day. Continue according to Step Two.

Fish Cakes

I LOVE THE FROZEN PACKAGES OF "VEGETABLE BLEND"—A COMBINATION OF CHOPPED ONIONS AND RED AND GREEN BELL PEPPERS.

SIDES: Sweet Marinated Slaw (page 144) and steamed green beans.

DESSERT: Frozen Raspberry Cream Pie (page 190).

MAKES 6 servings

- 1 cup frozen onions and bell peppers, thawed and finely chopped
- 16 ounces canned tuna or salmon, drained and flaked or crabmeat, drained, flaked, and cartilage removed
- ½ cup finely crushed saltine crackers
- ¼ cup finely chopped fresh parsley
- 2 large eggs
- 3 tablespoons fresh lemon juice
- 1 tablespoon Worcestershire sauce
- 1 teaspoon salt
- ½ teaspoon black pepper
- 2 tablespoons vegetable oil

  Purchased tartar sauce

ONE In a large bowl combine onions and bell peppers, tuna, crackers, parsley, eggs, lemon juice, Worcestershire sauce, salt, and black pepper. Form mixture into 6 patties, each about ½ inch thick.

TWO Preheat the oil in an extra-large skillet over medium heat. Add patties in a single layer; cook 3 to 4 minutes per side or until golden brown. If desired, serve with tartar sauce.

PLAN AHEAD: Prepare recipe through Step One. Cover and refrigerate up to 8 hours. Continue according to Step Two.

FREEZE AHEAD: Prepare recipe through Step One. Cover and freeze up to 1 month. Defrost completely in refrigerator. Continue according to Step Two.

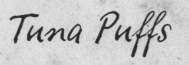

Tuna Puffs

THIS COMFORT FOOD IS PERFECT FOR A COZY SUPPER OR HEARTY SNACK YET IT IS DRESSY ENOUGH TO BE SERVED AT A LUNCHEON.

SIDE: Chop Chop Salad (page 201).

DESSERT: Pecan Fudge Cookies (page 186).

MAKES 3 servings

- 1   12-ounce can tuna, drained
- ¼   teaspoon Worcestershire sauce
- 2   tablespoons plus ½ cup mayonnaise
- 2   teaspoons Dijon mustard
- 2   teaspoons grated onion
- 2   tablespoons chopped green or red bell pepper
- 3   English muffins, split
- 6   thin tomato slices
- ½   cup finely shredded cheddar cheese

ONE In a large bowl combine tuna, Worcestershire sauce, 2 tablespoons of the mayonnaise, the mustard, onion, and pepper.

TWO Place English muffins, split sides up, on a baking sheet. Spread tuna mixture on muffins; top each with a tomato slice.

THREE Combine the remaining mayonnaise and the cheddar cheese. Spread mixture on top of each tomato slice. Broil sandwiches until topping is golden brown and puffy. Turn off broiler but keep oven door closed. Allow sandwiches to sit in the oven for 1 to 2 minutes before serving.

PLAN AHEAD: Prepare recipe through Step One. Cover and refrigerate up to 2 days. Continue according to Step Two.

vegetarian

Dilled Vegetables en Papillote

INSIDE FOIL PACKETS, HERBAL FLAVORS CONCENTRATE, WHICH PERFECTLY INFUSE THE VEGETABLES.

VEGETARIAN

SIDE: Golden Cheese Polenta (page 154).

DESSERT: Tuxedo Sundaes: Top scoops of vanilla ice cream with melted dark chocolate frosting and sprinkle with chopped cashews.

MAKES 6 servings

6	portobello mushrooms
6	12x12-inch foil sheets
6	sprigs fresh dill
1½	cups shredded fresh carrots
6	tablespoons finely chopped onion
6	tablespoons finely chopped red bell pepper
6	tablespoons sliced pimiento-stuffed green olives
6	tablespoons bottled Italian salad dressing

ONE Preheat oven to 375°F.

TWO For each packet, place 1 mushroom on a foil sheet. Top with a sprig of dill, ¼ cup carrots, 1 tablespoon onion, 1 tablespoon bell pepper, 1 tablespoon olives, and 1 tablespoon salad dressing. Bring top and bottom edges of foil together and fold down on top of vegetables. Tightly roll up side edges of foil, sealing packet.

THREE Place packets sealed sides up on large baking sheet. Bake 20 to 25 minutes. Let everyone open their own packets at the table. Warn diners to beware of hot steam when opening packets.

PLAN AHEAD: Prepare recipe through Step Two but don't preheat oven. Refrigerate up to 1 day. Preheat oven. Continue according to Step Three.

FREEZE AHEAD: Prepare recipe through Step Two but don't preheat oven. Freeze up to 1 month. Defrost completely in refrigerator. Preheat oven. Continue according to Step Three.

Caramelized Onions and Walnuts

THIS COMBINATION OF SWEET ONIONS AND CRUNCHY WALNUTS IS DELICIOUS AS A SPREAD OR AS AN ENTRÉE WHEN SERVED ON TOP OF BRUSCHETTA OR POLENTA.

SIDES: Crusty bread and Pearl Couscous Salad (page 199).

DESSERT: Lemon Herb Pound Cake (page 182).

MAKES 3 cups

- 6 **large onions, thinly sliced**
- 1 **tablespoon salt**
- ½ **teaspoon black pepper**
- 2 **tablespoons olive oil**
- ½ **cup chopped walnuts**

ONE In a large skillet cook onion slices, salt, and pepper in hot oil over medium heat for 45 minutes or until onion slices are caramel brown, stirring frequently (if onions begin to stick, reduce heat and cover pan).

TWO Add walnuts; cook and stir 5 minutes more.

PLAN AHEAD: Prepare recipe through Step Two. Cover and refrigerate up to 1 day. Reheat over low heat.

FREEZE AHEAD: Prepare recipe through Step Two. Cover and freeze up to 1 month. Defrost completely in refrigerator. Reheat over low heat.

Cannellini Beans, Tuscan-Style

LOTS OF GARLIC AND FLAT-LEAF PARSLEY ADD THE AROMA AND FLAVOR OF ITALY'S COUNTRYSIDE. TO BE REALLY AUTHENTIC, DRIZZLE EACH SERVING WITH OLIVE OIL.

VEGETARIAN

SIDES: Sliced ciabatta bread and tossed green salad with Italian dressing.

DESSERT: Raspberry Italian Ice (page 180).

MAKES 4 to 6 servings

- 1½ cups chopped onions
- 1½ cups chopped carrots
- 1 cup chopped celery
- 2 tablespoons chopped fresh garlic
- 2 tablespoons olive oil
- 3 15-ounce or two 19-ounce cans cannellini beans, rinsed and drained
- 1 cup chicken broth
- ¼ cup finely chopped fresh flat-leaf parsley
- 2 bay leaves
- 1 tablespoon chopped fresh thyme or 2 teaspoons dried thyme, crushed

    Salt and black pepper

ONE In a large saucepan cook onions, carrots, celery, and garlic in hot oil over medium heat until tender.

TWO Add drained beans, chicken broth, parsley, bay leaves, and thyme. Simmer, covered, 30 minutes. Season to taste with salt and pepper. Remove bay leaves before serving.

PLAN AHEAD: Prepare recipe through Step Two. Cover and refrigerate up to 3 days. Reheat over medium heat.

FREEZE AHEAD: Prepare beans through Step Two. Cover and freeze up to 2 months. Defrost completely in refrigerator. Reheat over medium heat.

Stuffed Roasted Peppers and Onions

A RIOT OF COLOR, THIS ENTRÉE IS ALSO A PARTY OF FLAVORS.

VEGETARIAN

SIDES: Cheddar Rice (page 130) and lemon wedges.

DESSERT: Cherry Meringue Cloud (page 172).

MAKES 6 servings

Nonstick cooking spray

1 15-ounce can garbanzo beans, rinsed and drained

12 cherry tomatoes, halved

1 cup prepared basil pesto

1 cup crumbled goat cheese or feta cheese

¼ cup sliced, pitted black olives

Salt and black pepper

3 medium red, green, and/or yellow bell peppers, halved and seeded

2 medium red onions, quartered lengthwise

4 medium tomatoes, halved

Olive oil

1 teaspoon salt

½ teaspoon black pepper

ONE Preheat oven to 400°F. Coat a large roasting pan with cooking spray; set aside.

TWO In a large bowl combine drained beans, cherry tomatoes, pesto, cheese, olives, and salt and black pepper to taste. Fill bell peppers with bean mixture; place in prepared pan. Arrange onion quarters and tomato halves around stuffed peppers. Drizzle with olive oil and sprinkle with the 1 teaspoon salt and the ½ teaspoon black pepper.

THREE Bake 30 minutes or until onions are tender and golden brown.

PLAN AHEAD: Prepare recipe through Step Two but do not preheat oven. Cover and refrigerate up to 1 day. Preheat oven. Continue according to Step Three.

Veggie Bean Taco Salad

PICK UP PREPARED VEGETABLES FROM THE DELI OR PRODUCE DEPARTMENT AND THIS BEAUTIFULLY ARRANGED SALAD IS A SNAP TO PREPARE.

SIDES: Warm corn tortillas and Chantilly Fruit Salad (page 137).

DESSERT: Sweet Brown Bread Sandwiches: Spread slices of brown bread (found in the baking aisle of the supermarket) with softened cream cheese.

MAKES 6 to 8 servings

- 1 15-ounce can pinto beans, rinsed and drained
- 1 4-ounce can chopped mild green chiles, undrained
- ½ cup salsa
- 1 1¾-ounce package taco seasoning mix
- ¼ cup water or chicken broth
- 1 10-ounce bag corn chips
- 1 head iceberg lettuce, shredded
- 1 small onion, thinly sliced
- ½ cup shredded carrot
- 1 medium tomato, chopped
- ½ cup chopped green bell pepper
- 2 cups broccoli florets
- 1 cup shredded cheddar cheese
- 1 cup sour cream
- 1 cup salsa

ONE In a large skillet heat drained beans over medium heat. Stir in undrained green chiles, the ½ cup salsa, taco seasoning, and water. Simmer, uncovered, 10 minutes.

TWO Meanwhile, on a large platter arrange corn chips. Top with bean mixture, lettuce, onion, carrot, tomato, bell pepper, broccoli, cheese, sour cream, and the 1 cup salsa.

PLAN AHEAD: Prepare recipe through Step One. Cover and refrigerate up to 2 days. Reheat over low heat. Continue according to Step Two.

FREEZE AHEAD: Prepare through Step One. Cover and freeze up to 1 month. Defrost completely in refrigerator. Reheat over low heat. Continue according to Step Two.

Gazpacho

BRIGHT, FRESH VEGETABLES WITH ALL OF THEIR VITAMINS EXPLODE IN THIS HEALTHFUL, TASTY SOUP.

SIDES: Pesto Bow Ties (page 132) and Garlic Pita Crisps (page 126).

DESSERT: Pecan Fudge Cookies (page 186).

MAKES 6 servings

- 5 medium tomatoes, peeled and coarsely chopped (2⅓ cups)
- ¼ coarsely chopped onion
- 1 teaspoon minced fresh garlic
- 2 small cucumbers, peeled and coarsely chopped
- ¾ cup coarsely chopped green bell pepper
- 1 46-ounce can tomato juice
- 2 tablespoons cider vinegar
- 1 teaspoon salt (or to taste)
- ½ teaspoon black pepper (or to taste)
- 2 drops Tabasco® (or to taste)
  Cucumber spears (optional)

ONE In a food processor combine tomatoes, onion, and garlic. Cover and process about 1 minute or until coarsely chopped. Transfer tomato mixture to a large bowl. In the food processor combine cucumbers and bell pepper. Process until coarsely chopped; add to tomato mixture in bowl. Stir in tomato juice, vinegar, salt, black pepper, and Tabasco.® Refrigerate 2 hours or until chilled.

TWO Serve in chilled glasses or bowls. If desired, garnish with cucumber spears.

PLAN AHEAD: Prepare recipe through Step One, except cover and refrigerate up to 1 day. Continue according to Step Two.

FREEZE AHEAD: Prepare recipe through Step One, except do not refrigerate. Cover and freeze up to 1 month. Defrost completely in refrigerator. Continue according to Step Two.

White Bean Chili

VEGETARIAN

WHAT COULD BE BETTER ON A COLD EVENING THAN A BIG BOWL OF CHILI? THIS VERSION IS BOTH HEARTY AND FRESH-TASTING.

SIDES: Garlic Pita Crisps (page 126) and Cran-Raspberry Molded Salad (page 136).

DESSERT: Pecan Caramel Pears: Drizzle drained, sliced, and warm canned pears with caramel topping and sprinkle with chopped pecans.

MAKES 6 servings

- 1 cup chopped onion
- ½ cup chopped green or red bell pepper
- ½ cup finely chopped carrot
- 2 tablespoons olive oil
- 3 15- to 16-ounce cans white kidney (cannellini) or navy beans, rinsed and drained
- 2 cups canned diced tomatoes, undrained
- 1 cup frozen corn
- 1 cup water
- 1 7-ounce can diced green chiles, undrained
- 2 vegetable bouillon cubes
- 2 tablespoons minced fresh garlic
- 2 to 3 tablespoons chili powder
- 2 teaspoons ground cumin

ONE In a 4- to 6-quart Dutch oven cook and stir onion, bell pepper, and carrot in hot oil over medium heat until tender. Stir in drained beans, undrained tomatoes, frozen corn, water, undrained green chiles, vegetable bouillon cubes, garlic, chili powder, and cumin.

TWO Simmer, covered, 30 minutes.

PLAN AHEAD: Prepare recipe through Step One. Cover and refrigerate up to 2 days. Continue according to Step Two.

FREEZE AHEAD: Prepare recipe through Step One. Cover and freeze up to 1 month. Defrost completely in refrigerator. Continue according to Step Two.

Sweet and Tangy Grilled Vegetables and Tofu

THIS SWEET-AND-SOUR MARINADE IS USED ON FLANK STEAK AT SUPER SUPPERS, BUT WE FIND IT WORKS INCREDIBLY WELL ON VEGETABLES AND TOFU AS WELL.

SIDES: Curried Rice (page 127) and tossed green salad.

DESSERT: Frozen Raspberry Cream Pie (page 190).

MAKES 6 servings

- 6 large portobello mushrooms
- 2 medium onions, cut into ½-inch slices
- 2 medium red and/or green bell peppers, cut into ½-inch slices
- 2 large zucchini or yellow squash, cut into 1-inch slices
- ⅓ cup soy sauce
- ⅓ cup packed brown sugar
- ¼ sliced green onions
- 1 tablespoon toasted sesame oil
- 1 tablespoon sesame seeds
- 2 teaspoons minced fresh garlic
- 1 teaspoon minced fresh ginger
- 2 12- to 16-ounce packages refrigerated water-packed firm or extra-firm tofu, drained and cut into ½-inch pieces

ONE Place mushrooms, onions, bell peppers, and zucchini in a resealable plastic bag set in a shallow bowl. For marinade, in a small bowl combine soy sauce, sugar, green onions, sesame oil, sesame seeds, garlic, and ginger. Pour over vegetables; seal bag. Refrigerate 1 hour, turning occasionally.

TWO Drain vegetables, reserving marinade. For a charcoal grill, grill vegetables on the rack of an uncovered grill directly over medium coals for 7 to 10 minutes or until tender, turning and brushing with marinade halfway through. For tofu, place a large piece of heavy-duty foil on the grill; top with tofu. Grill 7 to 10 minutes, turning and brushing with marinade halfway through. (For a gas grill, preheat grill. Reduce heat to medium. Place vegetables and tofu on heavy-duty foil on grill rack over medium heat. Cover; grill as above.)

THREE Meanwhile, in a small saucepan simmer reserved marinade 1 minute. Transfer cooked vegetables and tofu to serving platter and drizzle with marinade.

FREEZE AHEAD: Prepare recipe through Step One except use a freezer bag. Freeze up to 2 months. Defrost completely in refrigerator. (Vegetables may appear wilted but will grill fine.) Continue according to Step Two.

Bean and Noodle Casserole

THIS IS A GREAT CASSEROLE TO FREEZE AND TAKE ON A FAMILY SKI TRIP.
IT WILL DEFROST DURING THE CAR TRIP TO THE MOUNTAINS SO WHEN
YOU ARRIVE IT IS READY TO POP IN THE OVEN TO BAKE WHILE YOU UNPACK
THE CAR.

SIDES: Cheesy Corn Casserole
(page 167) and Texas Toast
(page 120).

DESSERT: Maui Sundaes: Top
scoops of vanilla ice cream with
sliced mangoes, pineapple tidbits,
and shredded coconut.

MAKES 6 servings

Nonstick cooking spray

- 1 cup chopped onion
- 1 cup chopped green bell pepper
- 1 teaspoon minced fresh garlic
- 1 tablespoon vegetable oil
- 1 12-ounce package dried thin egg noodles, cooked according to package directions
- 2 15-ounce cans pinto, black, or kidney beans, rinsed and drained
- 1 28-ounce can diced tomatoes, undrained
- 1 6-ounce can tomato paste
- 1 teaspoon salt
- ½ teaspoon black pepper
- 1 cup shredded cheddar cheese

ONE Preheat oven to 375°F. Coat a 2-quart baking dish with cooking spray; set aside.

TWO In a large skillet cook and stir onion, bell pepper, and garlic in hot oil over medium heat until onion is tender. Stir in cooked noodles, drained beans, undrained tomatoes, tomato paste, salt, and black pepper. Spoon mixture into prepared baking dish. Top with cheese.

THREE Bake 20 minutes or until heated through and cheese melts.

PLAN AHEAD: Prepare recipe through Step Two but don't preheat oven. Cover and refrigerate up to 2 days. Preheat oven. Continue according to Step Three.

FREEZE AHEAD: Prepare casserole through Step Two but don't preheat oven. Cover and freeze up to 1 month. Defrost completely in refrigerator. Preheat oven. Continue according to Step Three.

Bow Ties with Cheesy Steamed Vegetables

KIDS LOVE CHEESE AND GIVE THE STAMP OF APPROVAL TO THE FRESH VEGETABLES IN THIS DELICIOUS ENTRÉE.

SIDE: Parmesan Toasts (page 121).

DESSERT: Apricot Nectar Cake with Lemon Glaze (page 184).

MAKES 4 servings

Nonstick cooking spray

- 1 **12-ounce package dried bow tie pasta**
- 2 **cups coarsely chopped broccoli**
- 1 **cup thinly sliced carrots**
- 2 **cups fresh snow peas, trimmed**
- 1 **medium onion, sliced**
- 2 **tablespoons olive oil**
- 1 **teaspoon salt (or to taste)**
- ½ **teaspoon black pepper (or to taste)**
- 2 **cups shredded cheddar or Monterey Jack cheese**

ONE Preheat broiler. Coat a 13x9x2-inch baking dish with cooking spray.

TWO Cook pasta according to package directions. Place in prepared pan.

THREE Meanwhile, place broccoli, carrots, snow peas, and onion in a steamer; steam over 1 inch of water just until tender, about 7 minutes. Toss cooked vegetables with olive oil, salt, and pepper. Top pasta with vegetables; sprinkle with cheese.

FOUR Broil 3 to 4 inches from the heat until cheese melts.

PLAN AHEAD: Prepare recipe through Step Three but don't preheat broiler. Cover and refrigerate up to 8 hours. Preheat broiler. Continue according to Step Four.

Spaghetti Vegetable Pie

FROZEN VEGETABLES COME IN MANY INTERESTING COMBINATIONS. CHOOSE ONE YOUR FAMILY WILL LIKE.

VEGETARIAN

SIDES: Julie's Green Salad (page 147) and Texas Toast (page 120).

DESSERT: Pudding Parfaits: Layer pudding and thawed frozen fruit in parfait glasses. Top with whipped dessert topping.

MAKES 6 servings

Nonstick cooking spray

- 6 **ounces dried spaghetti**
- 2 **large eggs, beaten**
- 1 **tablespoon olive oil**
- ½ **cup grated Parmesan cheese**
- 1 **12-ounce package frozen mixed vegetables, thawed**
- 1 **roma tomato, thinly sliced**
- 1 **cup shredded cheddar cheese**

ONE Preheat oven to 375°F. Coat a 9-inch pie plate with cooking spray; set aside.

TWO Cook pasta according to package directions; drain. Return pasta to hot saucepan and keep warm. Stir in eggs, olive oil, and Parmesan cheese.

THREE Press pasta mixture into bottom and up sides of prepared pie plate, forming a crust. Layer mixed vegetables and tomato slices onto pasta crust. Sprinkle with cheddar cheese.

FOUR Bake for 20 to 25 minutes or until heated through and cheese melts.

PLAN AHEAD: Prepare recipe through Step Three but do not preheat oven. Cover and refrigerate up to 8 hours. Preheat oven. Continue according to Step Four.

FREEZE AHEAD: Prepare recipe through Step Three but do not preheat oven. Cover and freeze up to 1 month. Defrost completely in refrigerator. Preheat oven. Continue according to Step Four.

Twenty-Minute Skillet Lasagna

THE RAVIOLI'S PASTA AND CHEESE HELP FORM THE LASAGNA LAYERS.

SIDES: Sautéed Spinach and Pine Nuts (page 157) and Texas Toast (page 120).

DESSERT: Chocolate Ice Cream Pie: Spread softened chocolate ice cream in a 9-inch cookie crumb piecrust. Freeze until firm.

MAKES 4 servings

- 1   14-ounce jar spaghetti sauce
- 1   14½-ounce can diced tomatoes, undrained
- 1   pound refrigerated cheese ravioli
- 1½ cups ricotta cheese
- 8   ounces shredded mozzarella cheese

ONE In a medium saucepan combine spaghetti sauce and undrained tomatoes. Bring to a simmer over medium heat.

TWO Place 1 cup of the heated sauce in a large skillet. Arrange ravioli on the sauce. Spread ricotta on top of the ravioli. Top with remaining sauce.

THREE Simmer, covered, over low heat 10 minutes (do not stir). Uncover; sprinkle with mozzarella cheese.

PLAN AHEAD: Prepare recipe through Step One. Cover and refrigerate up to 2 days. Remove from refrigerator and let stand at room temperature for 30 minutes. Continue according to Step Two.

FREEZE AHEAD: Prepare recipe through Step Two. Cover and freeze up to 1 month. Defrost completely in refrigerator. Continue according to Step Three (may need to simmer longer than 10 minutes to heat through).

Mexican Pizza

A TORTILLA CRUST AND ZESTY MEXICAN FLAVORS MAKE THIS RECIPE SEEM LIKE A PARTY JUST WAITING TO HAPPEN.

SIDE: Cran-Raspberry Molded Salad (page 136).

DESSERT: Toasted Snowballs: Roll scoops of vanilla ice cream in toasted coconut. Drizzle with chocolate syrup.

MAKES 4 servings

- 2 10-inch flour tortillas
- 1 15-ounce can Mexican-style pinto or black beans, rinsed and drained
- 1 4-ounce can mild chopped green chiles, drained
- ½ cup sliced green onions
- 1 cup shredded cheddar or Monterey Jack cheese
- 1 cup salsa

ONE Preheat broiler.

TWO Place tortillas on a large baking sheet. Layer each with half of each of the drained beans, drained green chiles, green onions, and cheese.

THREE Broil 3 to 4 inches from the heat until cheese is melted. Cut into wedges and serve with salsa.

Frittata with Spinach and Tomatoes

LIKE QUICHE, THIS EGG ENTRÉE CAN BE EITHER ELEGANT BRUNCH FARE OR A COZY FAMILY SUPPER.

VEGETARIAN

SIDES: Curried Melon Salad (page 141) and Strawberry Bread (page 122).

DESSERT: Chocolate-Peanut Butter Ice Cream Cookies: Spread softened chocolate ice cream between peanut butter cookies. Freeze until firm.

MAKES 4 to 6 servings

- 4   large eggs, beaten
- 1   cup milk
- 1   cup shredded Monterey Jack cheese
- ¼   cup slivered fresh basil
- 1   teaspoon salt
- ½   teaspoon black pepper
- 1   cup chopped onion
- 1   tablespoon vegetable oil
- 1   10-ounce bag prewashed spinach
- 3   medium tomatoes, sliced
- ¼   cup grated Parmesan cheese

ONE Preheat oven to 375°F. In a large bowl combine eggs, milk, Monterey Jack cheese, basil, salt, and pepper; set aside.

TWO In a large ovenproof skillet cook onion in hot oil over medium-high heat until tender. Gradually add spinach to skillet; cook just until wilted. Stir in egg mixture. Cook until eggs are almost set but still moist, stirring constantly. Remove from heat. Arrange tomato slices on top. Sprinkle with Parmesan cheese.

THREE Transfer skillet to preheated oven. Bake frittata in skillet 5 to 6 minutes until set in center.

PLAN AHEAD: Prepare recipe through Step One. Cover and refrigerate up to 8 hours. Continue according to Step Two.

Judie's Cheese Quiche

EATING THIS QUICHE IS LIKE EATING BAKED, TOASTED CHEESE. YOU CAN USE WHATEVER CHEESE YOU HAVE ON HAND.

VEGETARIAN

SIDES: Chantilly Fruit Salad (page 137), Apricot-Walnut Scones (page 119), and Sautéed Red Cabbage (page 156).

DESSERT: Biscotti and spumoni ice cream.

MAKES 6 servings

- 4 to 6 cups shredded cheddar, Monterey Jack, and/or Swiss cheese
- 6 large eggs, beaten
- 1 teaspoon salt
- ½ teaspoon black pepper
  Milk, if needed
- 1 8- or 9-inch unbaked piecrust

ONE Preheat oven to 350°F.

TWO In a large bowl combine cheese, eggs, salt, and pepper. The mixture should be the consistency of cooked oatmeal; add a little milk if it is too stiff.

THREE Pour mixture into piecrust and bake 40 minutes or until a knife comes out clean when inserted near the center.

PLAN AHEAD: Prepare recipe through Step Two but do not preheat oven. Cover and refrigerate up to 1 day. Preheat oven. Continue according to Step Three.

FREEZE AHEAD: Prepare recipe through Step Two but don't preheat oven. Place egg mixture in freezer bag and freeze up to 1 month. Thaw in refrigerator. Preheat oven. Continue according to Step Three.

OPTION: Add black olives and chopped green chiles for Southwestern flair.

bread, grain & rice

Refrigerator Bran Muffins

WHEN RAISING THREE KIDS IT WAS ALWAYS
A SNAP TO BAKE A BATCH OF MUFFINS WHEN
I HAD THIS BATTER WAITING FOR ME IN THE
REFRIGERATOR.

MAKES 5 dozen muffins

- 6 cups All-Bran® cereal
- 2 cups boiling water
- 5 cups flour
- 2 cups sugar
- 5 teaspoons baking soda
- 1 teaspoon salt
- 1 cup vegetable oil
- 4 eggs
- 4 cups buttermilk
- ¾ cup raisins (optional)
- 1 cup chopped pecans (optional)
- 1 tablespoon orange zest (optional)

ONE In a large bowl combine 3 cups of the All-Bran cereal and the boiling water. Cover and let stand about 10 minutes or until most of the water is absorbed. In another large bowl stir together flour, sugar, baking soda, and salt. Beat in oil, eggs, and buttermilk with an electric mixer on medium speed. Stir in soaked cereal, the remaining 3 cups of the cereal, and, if desired, the raisins, pecans, and/or orange zest.

TWO Place in airtight containers and store up to 2 months in the refrigerator.

THREE To bake, preheat oven to 375°F. Line muffin cups with paper liners. Fill each muffin cup three-fourths full. Bake 20 minutes.

Stovetop Corn Bread

USING AN OLD-FASHIONED HEAVY OMELET PAN* ON THE STOVETOP SAVES HAVING TO TURN ON THE OVEN. THE BREAD STEAMS AND TURNS OUT MOIST.

MAKES 6 servings

Nonstick cooking spray

- 1 **cup cornmeal**
- 1 **cup flour**
- 2 **teaspoons baking powder**
- ½ **teaspoon baking soda**
- ½ **teaspoon salt**
- 1 **large egg**
- 1 **cup milk**
- ¼ **cup vegetable oil**

ONE Coat omelet pan with cooking spray; set aside.

TWO In a medium bowl combine cornmeal, flour, baking powder, baking soda, and salt. Make a well in the center and add egg, milk, and oil. Use a wooden spoon to mix well.

THREE Place prepared omelet pan on stove over medium heat. When pan is hot, pour corn bread batter into one side. Close pan; turn heat to low and cook 10 minutes. Open pan and use knife to loosen sides of bread; close pan and turn pan over. Cook 8 to 10 minutes on the second side or until bread is firm in the center.

PLAN AHEAD: Prepare recipe through Step Three. Cover and refrigerate up to 1 day. Reheat bread under broiler.

FREEZE AHEAD: Prepare recipe through Step Three. Cover and freeze up to 1 month. Defrost completely in refrigerator. Reheat bread under broiler.

*NOTE: WareEver® made this kind of pan in the 1950s. They also were called Camp Pans. Look for them at antiques stores or on web sites. They come in regular and large sizes. The large pan will hold all the batter at once. The small pan will hold half the batter, so you will need to bake in two batches.

Apricot-Walnut Scones

THE RECIPE FOR THESE DELECTABLE SCONES COMES FROM MY NIECE WENDY. WALNUTS AND APRICOTS GIVE THEM A CALIFORNIA FLAIR, WHICH IS WHERE WENDY LIVES.

MAKES 2 dozen scones

- 2 **cups flour**
- ⅓ **cup sugar**
- 2 **teaspoons baking powder**
- ½ **teaspoon salt**
- 1 **stick butter (½ cup), chilled and cut into 8 slices**
- ¾ **cup whipping cream**
- 1 **large egg**
- 2 **teaspoons vanilla**
- 1 **cup white chocolate chips**
- 1 **cup coarsely chopped walnuts**
- 1 **cup finely chopped dried apricots**

ONE Preheat oven to 350°F. Cover a baking sheet with foil. In a large bowl combine flour, sugar, baking powder, and salt. Add butter and use a pastry blender or 2 knives to cut in butter until mixture resembles coarse crumbs.

TWO In a small bowl combine cream, egg, and vanilla. Add cream mixture to flour mixture and stir with a fork until combined. Stir in chocolate chips, walnuts, and apricots.

THREE Drop by rounded tablespoons onto prepared baking sheet. Bake 15 to 20 minutes or until tops are light brown. Remove baking sheet from oven and let stand 5 minutes before removing scones.

PLAN AHEAD: Prepare scones. Place in an airtight container and store at room temperature up to 1 day. Reheat in a 350°F oven 5 minutes or until hot.

FREEZE AHEAD: Prepare scones; cool. Place scones in a freezer bag and freeze up to 1 month. Defrost completely. Reheat in a 350°F oven 5 minutes or until hot.

Texas Toast

HEARTY SLICES OF TOAST ARE COVERED WITH BITS OF GARLIC, A HINT OF CHILI, AND MELTED CHEESE.

BREAD

MAKES 4 to 6 servings

- 6 **slices thick-cut bread**
- 6 **tablespoons butter or olive oil**
- 1 **teaspoon minced fresh garlic**
- ½ **teaspoon chili powder**
- ½ **teaspoon seasoned salt**
- ¾ **cup cheddar cheese**

ONE Preheat broiler. Place bread slices on a baking sheet. In a small bowl combine butter, garlic, chili powder, and seasoned salt. Brush each bread slice with butter mixture.

TWO Broil 4 inches from heat 2 to 3 minutes or until toasted. Sprinkle each piece of toast with 2 tablespoons cheddar cheese. Broil 4 inches from heat until cheese melts.

PLAN AHEAD: Prepare recipe. Cover and store at room temperature for up to 1 week. Serve at room temperature or reheat under broiler.

FREEZE AHEAD: Prepare recipe. Cover and freeze up to 1 month. Defrost completely in refrigerator. Serve at room temperature or reheat under broiler.

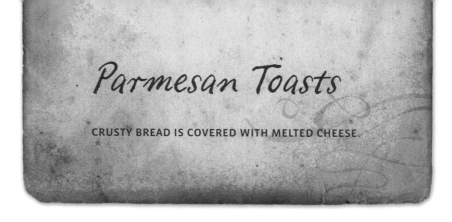

Parmesan Toasts

CRUSTY BREAD IS COVERED WITH MELTED CHEESE.

MAKES 4 to 6 servings

12 ½-inch slices baguette-style French bread

¼ cup olive oil

¾ to 1½ cups shredded Parmesan cheese

ONE Preheat broiler. Place bread slices on a baking sheet. Brush each bread slice with olive oil.

TWO Broil 4 inches from heat 2 to 3 minutes or until toasted. Sprinkle each piece of toast with 1 to 2 tablespoons Parmesan cheese. Broil 4 inches from heat until cheese melts.

PLAN AHEAD: Prepare recipe. Cover and store at room temperature for up to 1 week. Serve at room temperature or reheat under broiler.

FREEZE AHEAD: Prepare recipe. Cover and freeze up to 1 month. Defrost completely in refrigerator. Serve at room temperature or reheat under broiler.

Strawberry Bread

MY FRIEND CAROL ALWAYS SEEMS TO BE ABLE TO PRODUCE SOMETHING FABULOUS TO EAT AT A MOMENT'S NOTICE. ONCE SHE CALLED ME OVER FOR A QUICK CUP OF COFFEE. AS I WALKED INTO HER KITCHEN SHE WAS PULLING A LOAF OF THIS BREAD OUT OF HER OVEN. WHAT A GIFT—TO TREAT A FRIEND TO A CUP OF COFFEE AND JUST-BAKED STRAWBERRY BREAD.

BREAD

MAKES 1 loaf

Nonstick cooking spray

2 cups frozen whole strawberries, thawed

4 eggs

2 cups sugar

1¼ cups vegetable oil

3 cups flour

1 cup chopped pecans

1 teaspoon baking soda

1 teaspoon salt

1 tablespoon ground cinnamon

ONE Preheat oven to 350°F. Spray an 8x4x2-inch loaf pan with cooking spray; set pan aside. Cut up any large strawberries.

TWO In a large bowl beat strawberries, eggs, sugar, and oil with an electric mixer on medium speed.

THREE In a medium bowl combine flour, pecans, baking soda, salt, and cinnamon; stir into egg mixture. Pour into prepared loaf pan.

FOUR Bake 1 hour or until wooden toothpick inserted near center comes out clean. Remove from oven and let stand 5 minutes before removing from pan.

PLAN AHEAD: Bake bread. Cover and store at room temperature up to 3 days.

FREEZE AHEAD: Bake bread. Cover and freeze up to 1 month. Defrost completely in refrigerator.

TIP: To help bread come out of the pan easily, run a sharp knife along the outside of the loaf to separate it from the pan.

Croissant Stuffing

WHAT COULD BE MORE INDULGENT AND RICH THAN STUFFING MADE FROM BUTTERY CROISSANTS?

MAKES 8 servings

Nonstick cooking spray

- 8 croissants, torn into 1-inch pieces
- 1½ cups chopped celery
- 1 cup chopped onion
- 2 cups milk or chicken broth
- 4 eggs
- 3 tablespoons snipped fresh sage or 1 teaspoon dried sage, crushed
- 2 tablespoons snipped fresh thyme or 1 teaspoon dried thyme, crushed
- 1 teaspoon minced fresh garlic
- 1 teaspoon salt (or to taste)
- ½ teaspoon black pepper (or to taste)

ONE Preheat oven to 350°F. Coat a 3-quart baking dish with cooking spray; set aside.

TWO In a large bowl combine croissants, celery, onion, milk, eggs, sage, thyme, garlic, salt, and pepper. Transfer mixture to prepared baking dish.

THREE Bake 45 minutes or until golden brown.

PLAN AHEAD: Prepare recipe through Step Two but do not preheat oven. Cover and refrigerate up to 1 day. Preheat oven. Continue according to Step Three.

FREEZE AHEAD: Prepare recipe through Step Two but do not preheat oven. Cover and freeze up to 2 months. Defrost completely in the refrigerator. Preheat oven. Continue according to Step Three.

Deb's Bread

MY FRIEND DEBBY BROWN GAVE ME THIS
INCREDIBLE BREAD RECIPE. EACH BISCUIT IS
SO RICH, BUT IT IS HARD TO EAT JUST ONE.

MAKES 16 biscuits

Nonstick cooking spray

2   **cups Bisquick®**

½   **cup butter, melted**

1   **cup sour cream**

1   **tablespoon sesame seeds**

ONE Preheat oven 350°F. Spray a 9x9x2-inch square baking dish with cooking spray; set aside.

TWO In a large bowl combine Bisquick®, melted butter, and sour cream. Use a fork to stir mixture into a thick batter. Spread batter evenly in prepared baking dish; sprinkle with sesame seeds.

THREE Bake 30 to 35 minutes or until golden brown.

TIP: This recipe can easily be doubled or tripled.

Garlic Pita Crisps

USE SCISSORS TO CUT THROUGH THE OUTER EDGE OF EACH PITA TO PRODUCE TWO THIN LAYERS.

MAKES 4 to 6 servings

¼ cup olive oil

1 teaspoon minced fresh garlic

2 pitas, cut into 2 layers and then into triangles

1 tablespoon kosher salt

ONE Preheat oven to 375°F. In a small saucepan heat olive oil and garlic just until garlic starts to turn golden. Remove from heat.

TWO Place pita triangles on baking sheet and brush with the garlic olive oil. Sprinkle lightly with salt. Bake 5 minutes or until crispy.

PLAN AHEAD: Bake crisps. Cover and store at room temperature up to 2 days. Reheat under broiler.

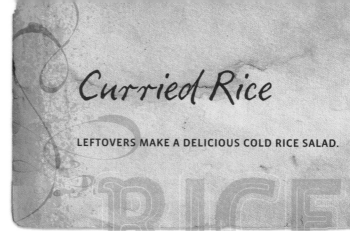

Curried Rice

LEFTOVERS MAKE A DELICIOUS COLD RICE SALAD.

MAKES 6 servings

Nonstick cooking spray

3 cups cooked white rice

1 cup chopped green bell pepper

1 2-ounce jar chopped pimiento

⅓ cup chopped green onions

¼ cup roasted peanuts

2 tablespoons raisins

¼ cup chopped fresh flat-leaf parsley

¾ cup olive oil

½ cup red wine vinegar

2 tablespoons fresh lemon juice

1 tablespoon grated fresh ginger

1 tablespoon Dijon mustard

1 teaspoon minced fresh garlic

1 tablespoon sugar

½ teaspoon curry powder

1 teaspoon salt (or to taste)

½ teaspoon black pepper

1 cup shredded cheddar cheese

ONE Preheat oven to 350°F. Coat a 3-quart baking dish with cooking spray; set aside.

TWO In a large bowl combine rice, bell pepper, pimiento, green onions, peanuts, raisins, and parsley. In a medium bowl whisk together olive oil, vinegar, lemon juice, ginger, mustard, garlic, sugar, curry powder, salt, and black pepper. Pour over rice mixture; toss to coat. Spread mixture in prepared baking dish.

THREE Sprinkle with cheddar cheese. Bake 20 to 25 minutes or until cheese melts.

PLAN AHEAD: Prepare recipe through Step Two but don't preheat oven. Cover and refrigerate up to 2 days. Preheat oven. Continue according to Step Three.

FREEZE AHEAD: Prepare recipe through Step Two but don't preheat oven. Cover and freeze up to 1 month. Defrost completely in refrigerator. Preheat oven. Continue according to Step Three.

Tabbouleh

MADE WITH WHOLE WHEAT GRAINS, THIS DISH IS BRIMMING WITH NUTRITION.

GRAIN

MAKES 6 to 8 servings

2   cups quick-cooking bulgur

2   cups cold water

¾   cup olive oil

¾   cup fresh lemon juice

1   cup diced tomatoes

½   cup chopped fresh flat-leaf parsley

1   teaspoon salt (or to taste)

½   teaspoon pepper (or to taste)

Pita bread

ONE In a large bowl combine bulgur with water. Stir in olive oil and lemon juice. Let stand 30 minutes or until water is absorbed.

TWO Add tomatoes, parsley, salt, and pepper; toss to coat. Serve at room temperature or chill overnight Serve with pita bread..

PLAN AHEAD: Prepare recipe. Cover and refrigerate up to 2 days.

Cheddar Rice

THIS DISH MAKES A FLAVORFUL CHANGE FROM MACARONI AND CHEESE, AND IT IS JUST AS KID-FRIENDLY.

MAKES 4 servings

Nonstick cooking spray

2 cups cooked white rice

2 cups shredded sharp cheddar cheese

2 cups sour cream

½ teaspoon salt

½ teaspoon white pepper

ONE Preheat oven to 300°F. Coat a 2-quart baking dish with cooking spray; set aside.

TWO In a large bowl combine cooked rice, cheese, sour cream, salt, and pepper. Spread in prepared baking dish.

THREE Bake 15 minutes or until heated through.

PLAN AHEAD: Prepare recipe through Step Two but don't preheat oven. Cover and refrigerate up to 2 days. Preheat oven. Continue according to Step Three.

FREEZE AHEAD: Prepare recipe through Step Two but don't preheat oven. Cover and freeze up to 1 month. Defrost completely in refrigerator. Preheat oven. Continue according to Step Three.

Maui Wild Rice Pilaf

THIS IS A GREAT SIDE DISH, BUT WE LOVE IT SO MUCH THAT IT COULD BE THE WHOLE MEAL. TANGY ORANGE MARMALADE, NUTTY RICE, AND SWEET COCONUT MAKE THIS PILAF A GREAT CHANGE OF PACE.

MAKES 6 servings

- ½ cup uncooked wild rice
- 2 cups water
- 1½ cups uncooked long grain rice, cooked according to package directions
- ½ cup toasted coconut
- ¼ cup chopped pecans
- 1 tablespoon orange marmalade
- 1 teaspoon grated orange zest
- ½ teaspoon ground ginger
- ½ teaspoon minced fresh garlic

ONE Combine wild rice and water in a saucepan. Bring to boiling; reduce heat to low and simmer, covered, 1 hour or until rice is tender. Drain any water remaining in pan.

TWO In a large bowl combine wild rice with cooked long grain rice, coconut, pecans, orange marmalade, orange zest, ginger, and garlic; toss to coat.

PLAN AHEAD: Prepare pilaf. Cover and refrigerate up to 1 day. Serve chilled or reheat in a 350°F oven for 20 minutes or until heated through.

FREEZE AHEAD: Prepare pilaf. Cover and freeze up to 1 month. Defrost completely in refrigerator. Serve chilled or reheat in a 350°F oven for 20 minutes or until heated through.

Pesto Bow Ties

PREPARED PESTO FROM THE GROCERY STORE MAKES THIS SIDE DISH A SNAP. IF YOU ADD CHOPPED, COOKED CHICKEN IT COULD BE AN ENTRÉE.

MAKES 4 to 6 servings

1   **pound dried bow tie (farfalle) pasta, cooked according to package directions**

1   **tablespoon olive oil**

½ to ¾ **cup prepared pesto (or to taste)**

¼   **cup chopped sun-dried tomatoes**

ONE In a large bowl toss cooked pasta with olive oil. Stir in pesto and tomatoes. Serve immediately or cover and refrigerate up to 1 day.

Lemon and Feta Orzo Salad

TINY, RICE-SHAPED PASTA, ORZO IS FUN TO EAT AND MAKES A UNIQUE SALAD.

MAKES 6 servings

- ½ cup olive oil
- ¼ cup fresh lemon juice
- 1 tablespoon finely chopped fresh dill
- 1 teaspoon grated lemon zest
- 2 teaspoons finely minced fresh garlic
- 1 teaspoon salt (or to taste)
- ½ teaspoon black pepper (or to taste)
- 1 pound dried orzo, cooked according to package directions and chilled
- ¾ cup crumbled feta cheese
- 1 cup finely chopped yellow bell pepper
- 1 cup finely chopped red bell pepper
- ½ cup kalamata olives
- ⅓ cup finely sliced green onions
- 1 teaspoon dried oregano, crushed

ONE In a large bowl whisk together olive oil, lemon juice, dill, lemon zest, garlic, salt, and black pepper.

TWO Stir in cooked orzo, feta cheese, yellow bell pepper, red bell pepper, olives, green onions, and oregano; toss to coat.

PLAN AHEAD: Prepare recipe through Step Two. Cover and refrigerate up to 4 hours.

salads

Cran-Raspberry Molded Salad

THIS CHERISHED SALAD IS GREAT ALL YEAR, BUT IT IS ESPECIALLY PLEASING WITH GRILLED CHICKEN AT SUMMER COOKOUTS.

MAKES 6 servings

- 1 **15-ounce can crushed pineapple, drained and juice reserved**
- 1 **3-ounce package raspberry gelatin**
- 1 **16-ounce can whole berry cranberry sauce**
- 1 **tablespoon grated orange zest**
- 1 **8-ounce can mandarin oranges, drained**
- 1 **cup whipping cream**

ONE In a saucepan combine reserved pineapple juice with water to equal 1 cup. Add gelatin; cook and stir until gelatin dissolves. Stir in drained pineapple, cranberry sauce, orange zest, and mandarin oranges.

TWO Pour mixture into a large bowl and chill 1 hour or until partially set. In a medium bowl beat whipping cream with an electric mixer on high until stiff peaks form. Fold whipped cream into gelatin mixture. Pour into a 6-cup mold. Refrigerate at least 4 hours before unmolding onto a serving plate.

PLAN AHEAD: Prepare recipe through Step Two but don't unmold salad. Cover and refrigerate up to 2 days. Unmold salad.

Chantilly Fruit Salad

MY DAUGHTER TERESA MAKES THIS SALAD TO SERVE WITH HOLIDAY DINNERS.

MAKES 6 servings

1   15-ounce can fruit cocktail in light syrup, drained

1   8-ounce can mandarin oranges, drained

1   cup grapes

2   cups sliced bananas, strawberries, and/or peaches

2   cups whipping cream

2   tablespoons powdered sugar

1   teaspoon vanilla

ONE In a large bowl combine drained fruit cocktail, drained mandarin oranges, grapes, and banana slices. In a medium bowl beat whipping cream, powdered sugar, and vanilla with an electric mixer on high until stiff peaks form.

TWO Gently fold whipped cream mixture into fruit mixture. Serve immediately.

Feta Cheese Potato Salad

I MADE THIS DOZENS OF TIMES WHILE RAISING MY KIDS.

MAKES 4 to 6 servings

- 3 **pounds new potatoes, unpeeled**
- **Salt**
- ¼ **cup fresh lemon juice**
- ½ **cup finely chopped pimiento or bottled roasted red bell pepper**
- 1 **cup sliced, pitted black olives**
- 1 **cup sliced green onions**
- 1 **tablespoon dried oregano, crushed**
- ½ **cup olive oil**
- ½ **cup vegetable oil**
- ½ **teaspoon salt (or to taste)**
- ½ **teaspoon black pepper (or to taste)**
- ½ **cup crumbled feta cheese**

ONE In a large saucepan boil potatoes in enough salted water to cover until tender. When cool enough to handle, cut potatoes into bite-size chunks; place in a large bowl. Sprinkle warm potatoes with ¼ cup of the lemon juice. Stir in pimiento, olives, green onions, and oregano.

TWO For dressing, in a small bowl whisk together the remaining ¼ cup lemon juice, the olive oil, vegetable oil, the ½ teaspoon salt, and the pepper. Drizzle dressing over potato mixture; toss gently to coat. Cover and refrigerate at least 2 hours. Just before serving, stir in feta.

PLAN AHEAD: Prepare salad. Cover and refrigerate up to 1 day.

Apricot Salad

**MY SISTER ANNE IS A GREAT COOK WHO ALWAYS
SEEMS TO HAVE SOMETHING YUMMY IN THE FRIDGE.
THIS IS ONE OF HER RECIPES.**

MAKES 12 to 16 servings

- 1 **20-ounce can crushed pineapple, undrained**
- 1 **6-ounce package apricot gelatin**
- 2 **cups buttermilk**
- 1 **12-ounce container frozen whipped dessert topping, thawed**

ONE In a saucepan simmer undrained pineapple for 5 minutes over medium-high heat. Turn off heat. Add gelatin; stir until dissolved. Stir in buttermilk.

TWO Pour into a 13x9x2-inch pan and refrigerate until cool but not set. Fold in whipped topping and refrigerate until firm.

PLAN AHEAD: Prepare salad. Cover and refrigerate up to 2 days.

TIP: Fat-free whipped dessert topping works well in this recipe.

Curried Melon Salad

IT'S WORTH THE EXTRA EFFORT OF MAKING THE MELON GLAZE—IT'S THE SECRET TO THIS REFRESHINGLY DELICIOUS SALAD.

MAKES 12 servings

6 cups finely chopped melon

⅓ cup red wine vinegar

1 teaspoon salt

½ teaspoon black pepper

1 teaspoon curry powder

3 tablespoons olive oil

1 small onion, thinly sliced

ONE For melon glaze, press 2 cups of the melon through a food mill or ricer. Discard the pulp and any seeds. Place all juices in a small saucepan. Bring to boiling; boil until reduced to ⅓ cup. Stir in vinegar, salt, pepper, curry powder, olive oil, and onion. Cook and stir 1 minute.

TWO Transfer melon mixture to a chilled bowl and chill in the refrigerator 4 hours or in freezer 30 minutes.

THREE Place the remaining 4 cups melon in a large bowl. Pour chilled melon glaze over melon; toss to coat.

PLAN AHEAD: Prepare salad. Cover and refrigerate up to 2 days.

Panzanella

I'VE BEEN HOOKED ON THIS SALAD SINCE THE FIRST TIME I ATE IT IN TUSCANY. USE TOUGH, DENSE BREAD LIKE THE ITALIANS DO. YOU'LL BE HOOKED AS WELL.

MAKES 4 servings

- 6 ripe roma tomatoes, halved
- 2 cloves garlic, slivered
- ¾ cup olive oil
- 4 ¾-inch slices dense bread, such as ciabatta or sourdough
- 1 medium cucumber, halved, seeded, and thinly sliced
- 1 cup chopped red onion
- 1 bunch fresh basil leaves, torn
- ¼ cup capers
- 2 tablespoons balsamic vinegar
- 2 tablespoons fresh lemon juice

  Salt and black pepper to taste

ONE Preheat oven to 350°F. Use a knife to make small slits in the tomato halves. Push 1 sliver of garlic into each slit. Place tomatoes, cut sides down, on a baking sheet. Sprinkle with 2 tablespoons of the olive oil. Bake 1 hour.

TWO Meanwhile, toast bread in a grill pan until charred with marks on both sides. Cut toasted bread into bite-size pieces. Place in a large bowl.

THREE Add tomatoes, cucumber, onion, basil, and capers to bowl. Sprinkle with the remaining olive oil, the vinegar, lemon juice, salt, and pepper; toss to combine. Allow to sit an hour at room temperature to develop flavors.

PLAN AHEAD: Prepare recipe through Step One. Cover and refrigerate up to 1 day. Continue according to Step Two.

Sweet Marinated Slaw

SHHH, KIDS LOVE THIS SALAD, SO DON'T SPOIL IT BY TELLING
THEM CABBAGE IS GOOD FOR THEM.

SALAD

MAKES 12 servings

1 **3-pound head green cabbage, thinly shredded**

1 **large green bell pepper, very thinly sliced or shredded**

1 **large onion, very thinly sliced or shredded**

2 **cups sugar**

1 **cup vegetable oil**

2 **tablespoons celery seeds**

2 **tablespoons salt**

ONE In a large bowl combine cabbage, bell pepper, and onion. Set aside.

TWO In a saucepan combine sugar, oil, celery seeds, and salt. Cook and stir over medium heat until the sugar is dissolved and the mixture is hot. Pour over the cabbage mixture; toss to coat. Cool slaw. Cover and refrigerate at least 4 hours before serving.

PLAN AHEAD: Prepare recipe. Cover and refrigerate up to 1 week.

Snow Pea Salad

EVERY TIME I MAKE THIS SALAD, I ADD SOMETHING DIFFERENT SUCH AS SLIVERED RED ONIONS, CANNED WATER CHESTNUTS, OR BEAN SPROUTS. YOU CAN DO THE SAME TO PERSONALIZE THIS SALAD.

MAKES 4 servings

- 1 pound fresh snow pea pods, trimmed
- ½ cup sliced radishes
- ¼ cup sliced green onion
- 3 tablespoons chopped fresh cilantro
- 1 tablespoon toasted sesame seeds
- 1 tablespoon minced or grated fresh ginger
- ½ teaspoon minced fresh garlic
- 1 tablespoon toasted sesame oil
- 1 tablespoon vegetable oil
- 1 tablespoon wine vinegar
- 1 teaspoon sugar
- 1 teaspoon salt (or to taste)
- ½ teaspoon black pepper (or to taste)

ONE Place snow peas in a microwave-proof bowl. Cover with water and microwave on 100% power (high) 2 to 3 minutes or until snow peas turn bright green. Drain hot water and stir in 2 to 3 cups ice. Immediately remove snow peas from ice and place on paper towels to drain.

TWO In a large bowl combine snow peas, radishes, green onion, cilantro, sesame seeds, ginger, and garlic. Drizzle with sesame oil, vegetable oil, and vinegar. Sprinkle with sugar, salt, and pepper; toss to coat.

PLAN AHEAD: Prepare recipe. Cover and refrigerate up to 8 hours.

Caesar Spinach Salad

THIS EASY-TO-TOSS-TOGETHER SALAD IS TOTALLY SATISFYING.

MAKES 6 servings

- ½ cup bottled Caesar salad dressing
- 2 tablespoons fresh lemon juice
- 1 16-ounce bag prewashed spinach
- 1 cup croutons
- ¼ cup shredded Parmesan cheese

ONE In a large bowl whisk together salad dressing and lemon juice.

TWO Add spinach to bowl; toss to coat. Add croutons and Parmesan cheese; toss to combine.

PLAN AHEAD: Prepare recipe through Step One. Cover and refrigerate up to 1 day. Continue according to Step Two.

Julie's Green Salad

MY NIECE JULIE MAKES THIS ROMAINE SALAD FOR ALL OUR FAMILY GATHERINGS.

MAKES 8 servings

1   head romaine or leafy green lettuce

2   cups shredded Swiss cheese

1   pound fresh mushrooms, sliced

1   cup toasted sliced almonds

1   recipe Balsamic Italian Dressing

ONE In a large bowl combine lettuce, cheese, mushrooms, and almonds. Just before serving, drizzle with Balsamic Italian Dressing; toss to coat.

BALSAMIC ITALIAN DRESSING: In a screw-top jar combine 1 envelope Good Seasons® Italian Salad Dressing Mix, 3 tablespoons balsamic vinegar, ½ cup vegetable oil, and 2 tablespoons fresh lemon juice. Cover and shake well.

PLAN AHEAD: Prepare dressing. Cover and refrigerate up to 1 month.

Field Greens with Oranges and Ginger Dressing

I LOVE THE MIX OF SWEET ORANGES AND ONIONS, AND THE GINGER DRESSING ADDS A PERFECT SPARK.

SALAD

MAKES 4 servings

- 1 8-ounce bag prewashed mixed greens
- 1 orange, peeled and sectioned, or one 15-ounce can mandarin oranges, drained
- ¼ cup sliced almonds or pine nuts
- ¼ cup thinly slivered red onion
- 2 tablespoons fresh lemon juice
- 1 tablespoon minced or grated fresh ginger
- 1 teaspoon Dijon mustard
- 2 tablespoons vegetable oil
- ½ teaspoon salt (or to taste)
- ½ teaspoon black pepper (or to taste)

ONE In a large bowl combine mixed greens, orange sections, almonds, and onion.

TWO For dressing, in a screw-top jar combine lemon juice, ginger, mustard, oil, salt, and pepper. Cover and shake well. Pour over the greens; toss to coat.

Corn and Black Bean Salad with Chili-Lime Dressing

THIS IS ALWAYS A POPULAR OFFERING AT SUPER SUPPERS. WE ADD TENDER COOKED CHICKEN BREAST FOR A HEARTY MAIN DISH.

SALAD

MAKES 6 servings

- ¾ cup olive oil
- ¼ cup fresh lime juice
- 2 tablespoons chili powder (or to taste)
- 1 teaspoon salt (or to taste)
- ½ teaspoon black pepper (or to taste)
- 3 cups frozen whole-kernel corn, thawed
- 1 15-ounce can black beans, rinsed and drained
- 2 large tomatoes, chopped
- ½ cup chopped fresh cilantro
- ½ cup chopped green bell pepper
- ⅓ to ⅔ cup thinly sliced green onions

ONE In a large bowl whisk together olive oil, lime juice, chili powder, salt, and black pepper.

TWO Stir in corn, drained beans, tomatoes, cilantro, bell pepper, and green onions; toss to coat.

PLAN AHEAD: Prepare recipe through Step Two. Cover and refrigerate up to 1 day.

TIP: This dish is delicious as a filling for tortillas, as a dip with chips or crackers, or hot as an entrée.

vegetables & fruit

Chef's Couscous

CHEF HEATHER KURIMA, ADMINISTRATOR OF OUR COOKING SCHOOL, THE CULINARY SCHOOL OF FORT WORTH, HAS THE INCREDIBLE ABILITY TO TASTE A RECIPE JUST BY READING IT. THIS MAKES HER OWN RECIPES QUITE INTERESTING, INCLUDING THIS ONE FOR COUSCOUS. SHE SAYS THAT WITH CHICKEN ADDED IT BECOMES A HEARTY MAIN DISH.

MAKES 4 servings

- 2 **cups dried couscous, cooked according to package directions**
- 1 **cup canned black beans, rinsed and drained**
- 1 **cup frozen corn**
- 1 **bunch cilantro, finely chopped**
- 1 **tablespoon minced fresh garlic**
- ¼ **cup olive oil**
- 1 **cup diced jicama (optional)**
- 1 **tablespoon grated lime zest**
- 2 **tablespoons fresh lime juice**
- 1 **teaspoon salt**
- ½ **teaspoon black pepper**

ONE In a large bowl combine cooked couscous, drained black beans, frozen corn, cilantro, garlic, olive oil, jicama (if desired), lime zest, lime juice, salt, and pepper. Refrigerate until serving time.

PLAN AHEAD: Prepare recipe. Cover and refrigerate up to 2 days.

Golden Cheese Polenta

MY MOM OFTEN MADE GRITS, TODAY CALLED BY A FANCIER NAME—POLENTA. SHE WOULD REFRIGERATE THE COOKED MIXTURE IN A LOAF PAN THEN CUT IT INTO SLICES AND FRY IT IN BUTTER UNTIL CRISPY AROUND THE EDGES. GREAT COMFORT FOOD AND NOW SERVED IN THE NICEST OF RESTAURANTS.

MAKES 8 slices

- 3½ cups water
- ½ teaspoon salt
- 1 cup coarse cornmeal
- 2 tablespoons butter
- ¼ cup Parmesan cheese
- 1 cup shredded mozzarella cheese
- 1 teaspoon minced fresh rosemary or ¼ teaspoon dried rosemary, crushed
- 1 to 2 tablespoons olive oil

ONE Grease the bottom and ½ inch up the sides of a 8x4x2-inch loaf pan; set aside.

TWO In a saucepan bring water and salt to boiling. Slowly add cornmeal, stirring constantly until mixture begins to pull away from sides of the pan, 5 to 7 minutes. Stir butter, Parmesan cheese, mozzarella cheese, and rosemary into polenta until butter is melted.

THREE Spoon polenta into prepared pan. Cover with plastic wrap and refrigerate 2 hours.

FOUR Preheat broiler. Carefully remove polenta from the pan. Cut into slices. Brush each slice with olive oil and place on a large baking sheet. Broil 4 inches from the heat until golden brown, turning once.

PLAN AHEAD: Prepare recipe through Step Three. Cover and refrigerate up to 1 day. Continue according to Step Four.

FREEZE AHEAD: Prepare recipe through Step Three. Cover and freeze up to 1 month. Defrost completely in refrigerator. Continue according to Step Four.

TO SAUTÉ POLENTA: In a large skillet heat 1 tablespoon olive oil and 1 tablespoon butter over medium heat. Add polenta slices and cook until golden brown, turning once.

Sautéed Broccolini with Lemon and Feta

A CROSS BETWEEN BROCCOLI AND CHINESE KALE, BROCCOLINI IS A BRIGHT GREEN VEGETABLE WITH TENDER STALKS AND SMALL BUDS. SOMETIMES IT IS CALLED BABY BROCCOLI.

VEGETABLES

MAKES 6 servings

- 2 **pounds broccolini, cut into 1-inch florets**
- 2 **tablespoons olive oil**
- 1 **tablespoon fresh lemon zest**
- 2 **tablespoons fresh lemon juice**
- 1 **teaspoon salt (or to taste)**
- ½ **teaspoon black pepper (or to taste)**
- ¼ **cup crumbled feta cheese**

ONE In a large skillet cook and stir broccolini in hot olive oil over medium-high heat 2 to 3 minutes or until bright green. Stir in lemon zest, lemon juice, salt, and pepper. Cook, covered, 1 minute more.

TWO Transfer mixture to serving platter; sprinkle with feta cheese.

PLAN AHEAD: Prepare recipe through Step One. Cover and refrigerate up to 2 days. Reheat over medium heat. Continue according to Step Two.

FREEZE AHEAD: Prepare recipe through Step One. Cover and freeze up to 1 month. Defrost completely in refrigerator. Reheat over medium heat. Continue according to Step Two.

Sautéed Red Cabbage

THE SHARP TANG OF GOAT CHEESE GOES PERFECTLY WITH RED CABBAGE.

MAKES 6 servings

- 2 tablespoons butter
- 2 tablespoons olive oil
- 6 cups coarsely chopped red cabbage (1 medium head)
- ½ cup chopped onion
- 2 tablespoons cider vinegar
- 2 tablespoons packed brown sugar
- 1 teaspoon salt (or to taste)
- 1 teaspoon black pepper (or to taste)
- 3 ounces crumbled goat cheese

ONE In a large skillet preheat butter and olive oil over medium-high heat. Add cabbage and onion. Sprinkle with vinegar; toss to coat. Cook, covered, stirring occasionally 5 to 7 minutes or until cabbage is crisp-tender. Stir in sugar, salt, and pepper; cook and stir 1 minute more.

TWO Transfer mixture to serving platter. Sprinkle with cheese.

PLAN AHEAD: Prepare recipe through Step One. Cover and refrigerate up to 1 day. Reheat over low heat. Continue according to Step Two.

Sautéed Spinach and Pine Nuts

BACON AND TOASTED PINE NUTS ADD INCREDIBLE TASTE TO MILD SPINACH. A GREAT DISH FOR FALL OR THANKSGIVING.

MAKES 6 servings

- 2 slices bacon or turkey bacon*, slivered
- ¼ cup pine nuts
- 1 teaspoon minced fresh garlic
- 2 1-pound bags prewashed spinach
- ½ teaspoon salt
- ½ teaspoon black pepper

ONE In a large skillet cook bacon until crisp. Drain, reserving 1 tablespoon drippings in the skillet; set bacon aside. Add pine nuts and garlic to skillet; cook and stir 1 minute or until pine nuts begin to brown.

TWO Add spinach to skillet; cook and stir until spinach is wilted. Stir in bacon, salt, and pepper.

*If using turkey bacon, add 1 tablespoon vegetable oil to skillet.

Sautéed Asian Vegetables

KEEP THE VEGETABLES CRISP TO MAINTAIN THEIR BRIGHT COLORS.

VEGETABLES

MAKES 6 servings

- 1 pound fresh snow peas, trimmed
- 1 large red bell pepper, thinly sliced
- 1 large onion, thinly sliced
- 2 teaspoons minced fresh ginger
- 1 teaspoon minced fresh garlic
- 1 tablespoon olive oil
- 1 tablespoon toasted sesame oil
- ½ medium head napa cabbage, shredded
- 1 teaspoon salt (or to taste)
- 1 teaspoon black pepper (or to taste)

ONE In a large skillet cook snow peas, bell pepper, onion, ginger, and garlic in hot olive and sesame oil over medium-high heat 2 minutes. Add cabbage. Cook and stir 3 to 4 minutes or until vegetables are crisp-tender. Sprinkle with salt and black pepper.

PLAN AHEAD: Wash and cut up vegetables. Cover and refrigerate up to 1 day.

Sautéed Zucchini with Walnuts

WALNUTS ADD NICE CRUNCH AND TOASTY FLAVOR TO ZUCCHINI.

MAKES 4 to 6 servings

- 3 medium zucchini, thinly sliced
- ½ teaspoon ground nutmeg
- 1 teaspoon salt (or to taste)
- 1 teaspoon black pepper (or to taste)
- 2 tablespoons olive oil
- 1 tablespoon butter
- ½ cup toasted chopped walnuts

ONE In a large skillet cook and stir zucchini, nutmeg, salt, and pepper in hot butter and olive oil over medium-high heat 6 to 7 minutes or until zucchini is tender. Stir in walnuts.

PLAN AHEAD: Toast walnuts. Cover and store at room temperature up to 3 days.

Tomatoes Stuffed with Creamed Spinach

BRIGHT RED AND GREEN COMBINE TO MAKE THIS A BEAUTIFUL DISH.

MAKES 4 servings

Nonstick cooking spray

2 10-ounce bags prewashed spinach

1 teaspoon minced fresh garlic

½ teaspoon dried thyme, crushed

4 ounces fat-free cream cheese, softened

2 tablespoons pine nuts (optional)

1 cup shredded Parmesan cheese

4 large tomatoes

ONE Preheat oven to 375°F. Coat an 8x8x2-inch square pan with cooking spray; set aside.

TWO In a large skillet cook and stir spinach, garlic, and thyme over high heat until spinach is wilted. Stir in cream cheese until melted (use a wooden spoon to break up cream cheese if necessary). Stir in pine nuts, if desired, and ½ cup of the Parmesan cheese.

THREE Slice ½ inch off the tops of tomatoes. Use a spoon to remove the pulp (if desired, reserve pulp for another use*) leaving shell intact. Divide the spinach mixture evenly among the tomato shells. Place in prepared dish. Sprinkle with the remaining ½ cup Parmesan cheese.

FOUR Bake 20 minutes or until bubbly and golden brown on top.

PLAN AHEAD: Prepare recipe through Step Two but don't preheat oven or coat dish. Cover and refrigerate up to 2 days. Preheat oven. Coat dish. Continue according to Step Three.

*Chop tomato pulp. Stir into soups or scrambled eggs or toss with a green salad.

Mashed Sweet Potatoes

EVERY BITE IS PERFECTLY SWEET AND GOOEY SINCE ALL THE INGREDIENTS ARE EVENLY MIXED IN.

VEGETABLES

MAKES 6 servings

- 4 large warm baked sweet potatoes
- ½ cup butter
- ¼ to ½ cup packed dark brown sugar
- 1 teaspoon salt (or to taste)
- 1 teaspoon ground cinnamon
- ½ teaspoon ground nutmeg
- 1 cup milk plus more if needed

Butter (optional)

Brown sugar (optional)

ONE Cut sweet potatoes in half; use a spoon to remove pulp. In a large bowl mash sweet potato pulp with a potato masher or beat with an electric mixer on low speed. Add butter, brown sugar, salt, cinnamon, and nutmeg. Gradually add milk to make the potato mixture light and fluffy.

TWO If necessary, transfer sweet potatoes to a 1½-quart casserole or baking dish and heat in a preheated 350°F oven 15 to 20 minutes to heat through. If desired, top with butter and sprinkle with brown sugar.

PLAN AHEAD: Prepare recipe through Step One. Cover and refrigerate up to 2 days. Reheat over low heat, adding more milk if needed.

FREEZE AHEAD: Prepare recipe through Step One. Cover and freeze up to 1 month. Defrost completely in refrigerator. Reheat over low heat, adding more milk if necessary.

Parmesan Tomatoes

MY FRIEND OLIVIA RAISED FIVE KIDS, AND WHEN THEY COME HOME WITH THEIR FAMILIES SHE COOKS HUGE DINNERS. THIS IS A RECIPE THAT COMES IN HANDY FOR CROWDS—JUST KEEP DOUBLING IT!

MAKES 4 to 6 servings

2 **large tomatoes, each cut into 6 slices**

½ **to 1 cup shredded Parmesan cheese**

ONE Preheat broiler. Place tomato slices on a baking sheet. Sprinkle each with 1 to 2 tablespoons Parmesan cheese.

TWO Broil 4 inches from the heat about 1 minute or until cheese melts.

PLAN AHEAD: Prepare recipe through Step One but don't preheat broiler. Cover and refrigerate up to 2 hours. Preheat broiler. Continue according to Step Two.

Grilled Onions with Balsamic Glaze

CARAMELIZED ONIONS ARE ACCENTED WITH A SWEET-AND-SOUR GLAZE.

VEGETABLES

MAKES 6 servings

- 2 **large red onions, sliced 1 inch thick**
- 2 **tablespoons olive oil**
- 1 **teaspoon salt (or to taste)**
- 1 **teaspoon black pepper (or to taste)**
- 1 **recipe Balsamic Glaze**

ONE Preheat a grill pan over medium-high heat.

TWO Brush onion slices on both sides with olive oil. Place onion slices on the grill pan; sprinkle with salt and pepper. Cook 5 to 8 minutes per side until onions are tender and golden brown.

THREE Transfer onions to a serving platter; drizzle with balsamic glaze.

BALSAMIC GLAZE: In a medium skillet combine ½ cup balsamic vinegar, 2 tablespoons packed brown sugar, and 2 tablespoons butter. Bring to a simmer over medium heat. Cook 15 to 20 minutes or until reduced by half.

PLAN AHEAD: Prepare recipe through Step Two. Cover and refrigerate up to 1 day. Reheat on grill pan over medium-high heat. Prepare Balsamic Glaze. Cover and refrigerate up to 1 day. Reheat over medium heat. Continue as directed in Step Three.

Arizona Potatoes

THESE INTERESTING POTATOES ARE
DELICIOUS ANYTIME—SERVE AT
BRUNCH WITH EGGS OR AT DINNER
AS A SIDE TO STEAK.

MAKES 8 to 10 servings

Nonstick cooking spray

6 **cups frozen loose-pack shredded hash brown potatoes, thawed**

½ **cup butter, melted**

2 **cups shredded cheddar cheese**

¼ **cup sliced green onion**

2 **cups sour cream**

1 **teaspoon salt**

½ **teaspoon black pepper**

ONE Preheat oven to 375°F. Coat a 13x9x2-inch baking dish with cooking spray; set aside.

TWO In a large bowl combine potatoes, butter, cheese, green onion, sour cream, salt, and pepper. Spread mixture in prepared baking dish.

THREE Bake 30 minutes or until potatoes are tender.

PLAN AHEAD: Prepare recipe through Step Two but don't preheat oven. Cover and refrigerate up to 2 days. Preheat oven. Continue according to Step Three.

FREEZE AHEAD: Prepare recipe through Step Two but don't preheat oven. Cover and freeze up to 1 month. Defrost completely in refrigerator. Preheat oven. Continue according to Step Three.

Cheesy Corn Casserole

MY SISTER BARBARA BRINGS THIS DISH TO FAMILY DINNERS, AND EVERYONE LOVES IT.

MAKES 6 servings

Nonstick cooking spray

- 2 **15-ounce cans cream-style corn**
- 1 **cup chopped onion**
- 1 **cup chopped green bell pepper**
- 1 **2-ounce jar chopped pimiento, drained**
- 1 **cup instant rice**
- ½ **cup milk**
- 1 **teaspoon salt**
- ½ **teaspoon black pepper**
- 1 **cup shredded cheddar cheese**

ONE Preheat oven to 350°F. Coat a 2-quart baking dish with cooking spray; set aside.

TWO In a large bowl combine corn, onion, bell pepper, drained pimiento, rice, milk, salt, and black pepper. Pour into prepared dish.

THREE Cover and bake 45 minutes. Remove from oven; top with cheese. Bake 5 minutes more or until cheese melts.

PLAN AHEAD: Prepare recipe through Step Two but don't preheat oven. Cover and refrigerate up to 1 day. Preheat oven. Continue according to Step Three.

FREEZE AHEAD: Prepare recipe through Step Two but don't preheat oven. Cover and freeze up to 1 month. Defrost completely in refrigerator. Preheat oven. Continue according to Step Three.

Baked Beans with Caramelized Onions and Orange Marmalade

A DELICIOUS TWIST ON CLASSIC BAKED BEANS.

MAKES 4 servings

- 4 slices bacon, slivered
- 3 medium onions, thinly sliced
- ¼ cup orange marmalade
- 1 teaspoon dried thyme, crushed
- 1 16-ounce can baked beans
- 1 tablespoon Dijon mustard
- ⅛ teaspoon black pepper

ONE In a large skillet cook bacon over medium heat until crisp; drain, reserving 1 tablespoon drippings in the skillet. Set bacon aside. Reduce heat to low. Add onions to drippings in skillet and cook 20 minutes, stirring often, until onions are golden brown. Stir marmalade into onions; cook and stir 1 minute or until marmalade is melted.

TWO Return heat to medium. Stir in thyme, beans, mustard, pepper, and bacon. Heat through.

PLAN AHEAD: Prepare recipe. Cover and refrigerate up to 2 days. Reheat over low heat.

FREEZE AHEAD: Prepare recipe. Cover and freeze up to 1 month. Defrost completely in refrigerator. Reheat over low heat.

Jacques Pepin's Cranberry Sauce

I LEARNED ABOUT THIS UNIQUE AND DELICIOUS RECIPE FROM MY FRIEND, FOOD EDITOR AMY CULBERTSON. JACQUES IS KIND ENOUGH TO LET ME INCLUDE IT HERE.

MAKES 2 cups

- 1 **12-ounce package fresh cranberries (3 cups)**
- 1 **lime, cut into fourths lengthwise and then into very thin slices**
- 1 **cup maple syrup**
- ¼ **teaspoon cayenne pepper**
- ¼ **teaspoon ground ginger**
- ¼ **teaspoon mace**

ONE In a medium saucepan combine cranberries, lime, maple syrup, cayenne pepper, ginger, and mace. Bring to a simmer over medium-high heat. Reduce heat to medium and simmer, stirring occasionally, 5 to 10 minutes or until cranberries pop. Serve warm or at room temperature.

PLAN AHEAD: Prepare recipe. Cover and refrigerate up to 3 days. Reheat over low heat.

desserts

Cherry Meringue Cloud

THIS RECIPE CAME FROM SUPER SUPPERS' FOOD STYLIST JAANNE LEIKAM. THIS MERINGUE CRUST IS THE BEST I'VE EVER TASTED.

MAKES 8 servings

- 3 egg whites
- 1 cup granulated sugar
- 15 saltine crackers, crushed
- 1 teaspoon baking powder
- 1 teaspoon white vinegar
- 1 teaspoon vanilla
- ½ cup chopped pecans
- 1 3-ounce package cream cheese, softened
- ½ cup powdered sugar
- 1 teaspoon vanilla
- 1½ cups whipping cream, beaten until soft peaks form, or 1½ cups frozen whipped dessert topping, thawed
- 1 21-ounce can cherry pie filling

ONE Preheat oven to 350°F. In a large mixing bowl beat egg whites with an electric mixer on high speed until stiff. Fold in granulated sugar, crushed saltines, baking powder, vinegar, vanilla, and pecans. Spread mixture into a 9x9x2-inch square pan. Bake 25 minutes. Transfer to a wire rack; cool completely.

TWO In a medium mixing bowl beat cream cheese, powdered sugar, and vanilla with an electric mixer until smooth. Fold in whipped cream. Spread on top of cooled meringue, leaving ½-inch rim around the edge. Spread pie filling on top. Refrigerate 3 to 4 hours.

PLAN AHEAD: Prepare recipe through Step One. Cover and store at room temperature up to 1 day. Continue according to Step Two.

Instant Banana Pudding

I MADE THIS DOZENS OF TIMES WHEN RAISING
MY KIDS; NOW I MAKE IT FOR MY GRANDKIDS.
I USE LOW-FAT OR FAT-FREE WHIPPED TOPPING.

MAKES 8 servings

1 **6-ounce package vanilla instant pudding mix**

1 **cup sour cream**

1 **8-ounce container whipped dessert topping, thawed**

1 **16-ounce package vanilla wafer cookies**

4 **bananas, peeled and sliced**

ONE Prepare pudding according to package directions. Fold in sour cream and whipped topping.

TWO Place a layer of vanilla wafers in the bottom of a clear bowl. Top with a half of the bananas and half of the pudding. Repeat layers, ending with a layer of pudding.

PLAN AHEAD: Prepare dessert. Cover and refrigerate up to 1 day.

Black Forest Trifle

USE A CLEAR GLASS BOWL TO SHOW OFF THIS
DESSERT'S LUSCIOUS LAYERS.

DESSERTS

MAKES 10 to 12 servings

1   prepared angel food cake

2   6-ounce boxes instant
    chocolate pudding mix

2   21-ounce cans cherry
    pie filling

4   cups whipped dessert
    topping

ONE Cut cake into bite-size cubes. Prepare pudding
according to package directions but fold in cake
cubes before the pudding sets up.

TWO Place half of the pudding mixture in a clear
glass bowl. Spread on 1 can of pie filling and 2 cups
of the whipped topping. Repeat layers. Refrigerate
2 hours or until mixture is set.

PLAN AHEAD: Prepare dessert. Cover and
refrigerate up to 1 day.

Baked Fruit

TOP THIS SIMPLE AND ELEGANT DESSERT WITH HEAVY CREAM, WHIPPED CREAM, OR CRÈME FRAÎCHE.

DESSERTS

MAKES 4 to 6 servings

- 2 tablespoons butter, melted
- 2 tablespoons packed brown sugar
- 1 teaspoon ground cinnamon
- 6 medium peaches, apples, or pears, cut in half and seeds removed

ONE Preheat oven to 375°F. In a 2-quart baking dish combine butter, brown sugar, and cinnamon. Place fruit halves, cut side down, on butter mixture.

TWO Bake 20 minutes or until fruit is soft. Brush with butter mixture after 10 minutes of baking. Serve warm or at room temperature.

FREEZE AHEAD: Prepare dessert. Cover and freeze up to 2 months. Defrost completely in refrigerator. Reheat in a 375°F oven 15 minutes or until hot.

Quick Fruit Crisp

FRUIT CRISP IS EASIER THAN EVER WHEN YOU START WITH CANNED PIE FILLING. BROWN SUGAR AND OATS GIVE THE CLASSIC CRUNCH.

MAKES 9 to 10 servings

Nonstick cooking spray

1 **21-ounce can apple, cherry, or blueberry pie filling**

½ **cup packed brown sugar**

½ **cup rolled oats**

½ **cup flour**

1 **teaspoon ground cinnamon**

½ **teaspoon ground nutmeg**

¼ **cup butter**

ONE Preheat oven to 375°F. Coat an 8x8x2-inch baking pan with cooking spray. Spread pie filling in bottom of prepared pan.

TWO For topping, in a medium bowl combine brown sugar, oats, flour, cinnamon, and nutmeg. Use a pastry blender or two knives to cut in butter until mixture resembles coarse crumbs. Drop topping onto pie filling.

THREE Bake 20 minutes or until topping is golden brown and filling is bubbly.

PLAN AHEAD: Prepare recipe through Step Two but don't preheat oven. Cover and refrigerate up to 1 day. Preheat oven. Continue according to Step Three.

FREEZE AHEAD: Prepare recipe through Step Two but don't preheat oven. Cover and freeze up to 1 month. Defrost completely in refrigerator. Preheat oven. Continue according to Step Three.

Apple Dumplings with Cinnamon Sauce

HERE'S MORE COMFORT FOOD—CINNAMONY APPLES ENCASED
IN A GOLDEN PASTRY AND DRENCHED WITH SYRUP.

MAKES 9 to 10 servings

Nonstick cooking spray

3 tablespoons butter, softened

1½ cups sugar

¼ cup chopped pecans

¼ cup raisins

2 tablespoons ground cinnamon

3 prepared piecrusts

6 medium baking apples, cored but not peeled

1 large egg beaten with 1 tablespoon water to make a glaze

½ cup water

ONE Preheat oven to 375°F. Coat a 2-quart baking dish with cooking spray; set aside.

TWO In a large mixing bowl beat the butter and ½ cup of the sugar with an electric mixer on high until smooth. Stir in pecans, raisins, and 1 tablespoon of the cinnamon; set aside.

THREE Using a sharp knife, cut piecrusts into six 6-inch squares. Place an apple on each pastry square. Fill apple centers with butter mixture. Moisten edges of each pastry square with water; gather corners over apples. Pinch to seal. Place dumplings in prepared baking dish and brush with egg glaze.

FOUR Bake, uncovered, 25 to 30 minutes or until apples are tender.

FIVE Meanwhile, for sauce, in a small saucepan combine the remaining 1 cup sugar, the remaining 1 tablespoon cinnamon, and the water. Bring to a boil and simmer 5 minutes. Pour sauce over dumplings just before serving.

FREEZE AHEAD: Prepare recipe through Step Three but don't preheat oven and don't brush with egg glaze. Cover and freeze up to 1 month. Defrost completely in refrigerator. Preheat oven and brush dumplings with egg glaze. Continue according to Step Four.

Raspberry Italian Ice

NOW YOU CAN MAKE ITALY'S FAVORITE DESSERT, GELATO, AT HOME.

DESSERTS

MAKES 1 quart

- **2 cups frozen raspberries, partially thawed but not drained, or fresh raspberries**
- **1½ cups water**
- **½ cup honey**
- **2 tablespoons fresh lemon juice**

ONE Place raspberries, water, honey, and lemon juice in a blender. Blend on high until pureed and creamy.

TWO Transfer to an ice cream maker and freeze according to manufacturer's directions.

FREEZE AHEAD: Prepare dessert. Cover and freeze up to 1 week.

Chocolate Toffee Matzos

WHETHER YOU CELEBRATE PASSOVER OR NOT, THIS TRADITIONAL HOLIDAY TREAT FROM MY FRIEND JUDE SLOTER IS SURE TO BECOME A FAMILY FAVORITE.

MAKES 12 large matzos

½ pound matzos (about 8)

1 cup butter

1 cup packed brown sugar

2 cups chocolate chips (semisweet, milk, or white), peanut butter chips, or butterscotch chips

Nuts, sprinkles, and/or chocolate pieces

ONE Preheat oven to 350°F. Line a cookie sheet with foil and place matzos on foil, breaking if necessary to fill the sheet.

TWO In a small saucepan melt butter over low heat. Add brown sugar; cook and stir for 1 to 2 minutes or until mixture coats the back of a spoon. Brush matzos with brown sugar mixture.

THREE Bake matzos for 3 to 4 minutes or until glaze begins to bubble. (Watch carefully to prevent burning.) Remove from oven and sprinkle with chocolate chips. Return to oven and bake until chips begin to melt. Remove from oven and spread melted chocolate to cover matzos. Sprinkle with nuts. Freeze until hard. Break into pieces to serve.

FREEZE AHEAD: Prepare matzos. Cover and freeze up to 1 month.

Lemon Herb Pound Cake

PRETTY AND ELEGANT, THIS CAKE IS FULL OF LEMONY FLAVOR.

MAKES 12 servings

Nonstick cooking spray

Flour

- 1 cup butter
- 2 cups granulated sugar
- 4 large eggs
- 2½ cups flour
- 2 teaspoons baking powder
- 1 teaspoon salt
- 1 cup milk
- ½ cup grated lemon zest
- 3 tablespoons finely chopped fresh mint or lemon balm
- 1 cup chopped pecans (optional)
- ½ cup granulated sugar
- ¾ cup fresh lemon juice

Sifted powdered sugar

ONE Preheat oven to 325°F. Coat a fluted tube pan with cooking spray and dust lightly with flour; set aside.

TWO In a large mixing bowl beat butter and the 2 cups granulated sugar with an electric mixer on medium-high until smooth. Add eggs, one at a time, beating well after each addition.

THREE In a medium bowl combine the 2½ cups flour, the baking powder, and salt. Stir flour mixture into butter mixture. Beat in milk, lemon zest, and mint with electric mixer until smooth. If desired, stir in pecans. Spread batter evenly in prepared pan.

FOUR Bake 50 to 60 minutes or until a wooden toothpick inserted near center comes out clean.

FIVE Meanwhile, in a small bowl combine the ½ cup granulated sugar and lemon juice (don't worry if all the sugar doesn't dissolve). Pour lemon mixture over the top of the hot cake. Cool cake in pan 15 minutes. Remove from pan; cool completely. Sprinkle with powdered sugar.

PLAN AHEAD: Prepare cake. Cover and store at room temperature up to 1 day.

FREEZE AHEAD: Bake cake but do not sprinkle with powdered sugar. Cover and freeze up to 1 month. Defrost completely in refrigerator. Sprinkle with powdered sugar.

Apricot Nectar Cake with Lemon Glaze

THIS VINTAGE CAKE IS FROM THE 1950S. MY MOM MADE IT FREQUENTLY WHEN I WAS GROWING UP.

MAKES 12 servings

Nonstick cooking spray

1 2-layer size yellow cake mix

2 large eggs, separated

¾ cup vegetable oil

1 5½-ounce can apricot nectar

2 tablespoons fresh lemon juice

2 cups sifted powdered sugar

2 tablespoons fresh lemon juice plus more as needed

ONE Preheat oven to 350°F. Coat a fluted tube pan with cooking spray; set aside.

TWO In a large mixing bowl beat cake mix, egg yolks, oil, apricot nectar, and 2 tablespoons lemon juice with an electric mixer 2 minutes or until smooth. Scrape sides of bowl occasionally.

THREE In a medium mixing bowl beat egg whites until stiff peaks form. Fold egg whites into batter. Pour batter into prepared pan. Bake 45 minutes.

FOUR Meanwhile, beat powdered sugar and 2 tablespoons lemon juice with an electric mixer until the consistency of syrup. Add additional lemon juice, if necessary.

FIVE Remove cake from pan. Pour lemon glaze on the hot cake.

PLAN AHEAD: Prepare cake. Cover and store at room temperature up to 1 day.

FREEZE AHEAD: Prepare cake. Cover and freeze up to 1 month. Defrost completely in refrigerator.

Crazy Chocolate Cake

THE CAKE IS MIXED TOGETHER IN THE BAKING PAN, AND THE FROSTING REQUIRES ONLY A SAUCEPAN. MAKE THIS CAKE WHEN TIME IS SHORT.

DESSERTS

MAKES 12 servings

- 3 **cups flour**
- 2 **cups sugar**
- ¾ **cup unsweetened cocoa powder**
- 2 **teaspoons baking soda**
- 1 **teaspoon ground cinnamon**
- 1 **teaspoon salt**
- 1 **teaspoon vanilla**
- 1 **tablespoon vinegar**
- 5 **tablespoons vegetable oil**
- 1½ **cups water**
- 1 **recipe Chocolate Icing**

  Chopped pecans (optional)

ONE Preheat oven to 350°F. In a 13x9x2-inch baking pan, combine the flour, sugar, cocoa powder, baking soda, cinnamon, and salt. Use a spoon to make 3 wells in the flour mixture. Pour vanilla into the first well, vinegar into the second well, and oil into the third well. Pour the water over all, ½ cup at a time, mixing well after each addition.

TWO Bake 35 to 40 minutes or until a wooden toothpick inserted near the center comes out clean. Spread warm chocolate icing over warm cake. If desired, sprinkle with pecans.

CHOCOLATE ICING: In a saucepan heat ½ cup butter and 3 tablespoons cocoa powder until butter melts. Stir in 1 pound sifted powdered sugar, 1 teaspoon vanilla, and ¼ teaspoon salt. Add ¼ to ⅓ cup milk or enough to make spreading consistency.

PLAN AHEAD: Prepare cake. Cover and refrigerate up to 2 days.

FREEZE AHEAD: Prepare cake. Cover and freeze up to 1 month. Defrost completely in refrigerator.

Pecan Fudge Cookies

MY PERSONAL TRAINER, DANIEL MYERS, HAS A MOM
WHO COOKS ALL KINDS OF FABULOUS FOOD.
GLORIA MYERS GAVE ME THE RECIPE FOR THESE ULTRARICH,
DECADENT MORSELS.

MAKES 3 dozen cookies

- 2 **cups semisweet chocolate chips**
- 4 **egg whites**
- 1 **teaspoon vanilla**
- 1 **teaspoon cider vinegar**
- ¼ **teaspoon salt**
- 1 **cup shredded coconut**
- 1 **cup chopped pecans**

ONE Preheat oven to 350°F. Coat a cookie sheet with cooking spray; set aside.

TWO In a small saucepan cook and stir chocolate chips over low heat until melted; set aside to cool.

THREE In a medium mixing bowl beat egg whites with an electric mixer on high speed until stiff peaks form. Beat in vanilla, vinegar, and salt. Fold in melted chocolate until well blended. Fold in coconut and pecans.

FOUR Drop cookie batter by rounded teaspoons onto prepared cookie sheet. Bake 8 to 10 minutes or until cookies puff and start to show small cracks on top. Transfer to a wire rack; cool.

PLAN AHEAD: Prepare cookies. Cover and store at room temperature up to 3 days.

FREEZE AHEAD: Prepare cookies. Cover and freeze up to 1 month.

Chocolate Cream Cheese Pie

THIS INCREDIBLY EASY PIE TASTES AND LOOKS LIKE IT TOOK HOURS TO MAKE.

MAKES 8 servings

- **3** large eggs
- **2** 8-ounce packages cream cheese, softened
- **¾** cup sugar
- **½** teaspoon vanilla
- **½** cup semisweet chocolate chips, melted
- **1** 9-inch graham cracker piecrust

ONE Preheat oven to 325°F. In a large mixing bowl beat eggs, cream cheese, sugar, and vanilla with an electric mixer until smooth. Fold in melted chocolate. Pour into piecrust.

TWO Bake 30 minutes. Cool completely. Cover and refrigerate at least 2 hours.

PLAN AHEAD: Prepare pie. Cover and refrigerate up to 3 days.

FREEZE AHEAD: Prepare pie. Cover and freeze up to 1 month. Defrost completely in refrigerator.

Frozen Banana Split Pie

THIS PIE HAS ALL THE FLAVORS OF THE CLASSIC DESSERT. THE SLICES ARE BEAUTIFULLY LAYERED.

DESSERTS

MAKES 6 to 8 servings

- 1 **pint chocolate ice cream, softened**
- 1 **9-inch chocolate-cookie crumb piecrust**
- 1 **banana, peeled and thinly sliced**
- ¼ **cup strawberry jam**
- 1 **pint strawberry ice cream, softened**
- ⅓ **cup drained crushed pineapple**
- 1 **pint vanilla ice cream, softened**
- ½ **cup chocolate fudge sauce**
- 1 **cup whipping cream, beaten until stiff peaks form**
- 2 **tablespoons chopped pecans or other nuts**

Maraschino cherries (optional)

ONE Spread chocolate ice cream over crust, mounding in the center. Top with banana slices and strawberry jam. Freeze until firm.

TWO Remove pie from freezer and spread with strawberry ice cream, mounding in the center, and drained pineapple. Freeze until firm.

THREE Remove pie from freezer and spread with vanilla ice cream, mounding in the center, and fudge sauce. Freeze until firm.

FOUR Remove pie from freezer and spread with whipped cream; sprinkle with nuts and, if desired, cherries.

FREEZE AHEAD: Prepare pie. Cover and freeze up to 3 days.

Frozen Raspberry Cream Pie

JUST STIR TOGETHER, PILE INTO THE CRUST, AND FREEZE—WHAT COULD BE EASIER?

MAKES 6 servings

- 2 cups whipping cream, beaten until stiff peaks form, or one 12-ounce container frozen whipped dessert topping, thawed
- 12 ounces raspberry yogurt
- 6 ounces fresh or frozen and thawed raspberries
- 1 9-inch cookie-crumb crust

ONE In a large bowl combine whipped cream and yogurt. Fold in berries. Pour into crust.

TWO Freeze until serving time.

FREEZE AHEAD: Prepare pie. Cover and freeze up to 1 month.

Million Dollar Cream Pie

CREAMY, FRUITY FILLING GOES WELL WITH EITHER GRAHAM CRACKER OR CHOCOLATE COOKIE CRUST.

MAKES 16 servings

- 1 **20-ounce can crushed pineapple, drained**
- 1 **cup whipping cream, beaten until stiff peaks form, or one 8-ounce container frozen whipped dessert topping, thawed**
- ⅓ **cup fresh lemon juice**
- 1 **14-ounce can sweetened condensed milk**
- 1 **cup chopped pecans**
- 2 **9-inch graham cracker crusts**

ONE In a large bowl combine drained pineapple, whipped cream, lemon juice, sweetened condensed milk, and pecans. Spread in crusts. Refrigerate at least 1 hour or until firm.

PLAN AHEAD: Prepare pie. Cover and refrigerate up to 1 day.

Best-Ever Pumpkin Pie

A TOUCH OF MOLASSES GIVES THIS PIE A DEEP, RICH TASTE. SERVE COLD WITH WHIPPED CREAM.

MAKES 8 servings

- 1 **15-ounce can pumpkin**
- 3 **large eggs, beaten**
- 1 **12-ounce can evaporated milk**
- ⅓ **cup sugar**
- 2 **tablespoons molasses**
- 1½ **teaspoons ground cinnamon**
- ½ **teaspoon ground ginger**
- ½ **teaspoon salt**
- ¼ **teaspoon ground nutmeg**
- 1 **9-inch unbaked piecrust**

Sweetened whipped cream (optional)

ONE Preheat oven to 425°F. In a large bowl combine pumpkin, eggs, evaporated milk, sugar, molasses, cinnamon, ginger, salt, and nutmeg. Pour pumpkin mixture into piecrust.

TWO Place pie on a baking sheet. Bake 15 minutes. Reduce oven temperature to 350°F. Bake another 40 minutes or until a knife inserted in the center of pie comes out clean. Cool on a wire rack. If desired, serve with whipped cream.

PLAN AHEAD: Prepare pie. Cover and refrigerate up to 2 days.

FREEZE AHEAD: Prepare pie. Cover and freeze up to 1 month. Defrost completely in refrigerator.

Caramel Sauce

TOP ICE CREAM, CAKE, OR FRUIT WITH THIS
CLASSIC HOMEMADE SAUCE.

MAKES 3 cups

- 2 **cups packed brown sugar**
- 1 **cup butter**
- 1 **cup light corn syrup**
- ¼ **cup whipping cream**
- 1 **teaspoon vanilla**
- ¼ **teaspoon salt**

ONE In a saucepan combine brown sugar and ½ cup
of the butter. Bring to boiling over medium heat.
Whisk in corn syrup and cream. Reduce heat to low;
simmer 3 minutes.

TWO Remove from heat and whisk in the remaining
½ cup butter, the vanilla, and salt.

PLAN AHEAD: Prepare sauce. Cover and refrigerate
up to 2 weeks. Reheat in microwave.

gatherings

Do you ever have fleeting ideas of inviting friends, family, or neighbors over for a great-tasting meal and a fun, casual gathering? There is nothing like the intimate setting of home to create a relaxing ambience for an enjoyable meal and peaceful, uninterrupted conversation. Yet most of us aren't comfortable with the thought of planning, preparing, and serving company-worthy food.

Even in the midst of the business of life, at-home gatherings are not only possible but can be time-friendly, easy, and simple. With these meal plans and party tips, you won't have to give up vacation time to pull it off.

This chapter features complete plans for three fun events. Of course, the recipes can be interchanged, and each plan can be tailored for various occasions.

The foods included in these menus are designed to be kid- and adult-pleasing, light on prep time, and hardy enough to hold up well during lengthy events. Here are a few party hints to spark ideas and spur you to action.

✦ Choose a few items that you will make yourself, then purchase the rest or have guests bring them.

✦ Always select dishes that don't take extra time or attention at the last minute.

✦ Set the table and gather serving platters and dishes ahead of time to avoid last-minute searching and shuffling.

Backyard Get-Togethers

There are myriad reasons to gather friends and family together for an informal backyard party. Welcome new neighbors with a meet-and-greet theme. Assign a recipe to each guest and ask them to bring that dish.

This party can easily be adapted to celebrate July 4th. Just add red, white, and blue decorations. You might purchase a frosted sheet cake and decorate the top with blueberries and strawberries in an Old Glory theme.

This menu includes our incredible Super Suppers Asian Flank Steak, which you can either cook on your backyard grill or inside on the stovetop. The salads are fun for kids, yet appeal to adults. Two of them can be served cold for a summer cookout or warm for a fall theme.

The Party Plan

MENU
Super Suppers Asian Flank Steak
Pearl Couscous Salad
Chop Chop Salad
Cherry Tomato Salad
Garlic Bread (purchased)
Ice Cream Sundaes

1 WEEK AHEAD
+ Plan table seating, place settings, and centerpieces.
+ Check grill; replace fuel if needed.
+ Grocery shop for all but perishables.
+ Follow Freeze Ahead tip for flank steak.
+ Prepare Chop Chop and Couscous salad dressings; cover and refrigerate.

2 DAYS AHEAD
+ Count out plates, dessert bowls, cutlery, napkins, and drinking glasses.
+ Set steak in refrigerator to defrost.
+ Grocery shop for perishables.

1 DAY AHEAD
+ Prepare all salads according to plan-ahead directions.

DAY OF PARTY
+ Set tables. Set out and label serving platters.
+ Last preparation of food: toss Chop Chop Salad, grill steak, prepare Cherry Tomato Salad if serving warm, warm garlic bread.

BACKYARD FUN
+ Plan a treasure hunt. Write and hide clues that take your guests from one location to another in your yard. Hide a bag of fun little gifts at the end.
+ Hang a piñata from a tree. Piñatas don't have to be saved for birthdays!

Super Suppers
Asian Flank Steak

THE SECRET TO A TENDER, JUICY STEAK IS TO TAKE IT OFF THE HEAT AT MEDIUM-RARE AND THINLY SLICE IT ACROSS THE GRAIN. THIS SWEET AND ZESTY MARINADE IS PERFECT FOR A HEARTY STEAK.

MAKES 6 to 8 servings

- 1   2 to 2½-pound beef flank steak
- ½   cup soy sauce
- ¼   cup packed brown sugar
- 1   tablespoon toasted sesame oil
- ¼   cup sliced green onion
- 1   tablespoon sesame seeds
- 2   teaspoons minced fresh garlic
- 1   tablespoon grated fresh ginger

ONE Place flank steak in a resealable plastic bag set in a shallow bowl.

TWO For marinade, in a bowl stir together soy sauce, brown sugar, sesame oil, green onion, sesame seeds, garlic, and ginger. Pour marinade over steak; seal bag. Marinate in the refrigerator for 1 to 12 hours, turning bag occasionally. Drain steak, reserving the marinade.

THREE For a charcoal grill, grill steak on the rack of an uncovered grill directly over medium coals for 10 to 16 minutes for medium-rare doneness (145°F), turning and brushing once with marinade halfway through grilling. (For a gas grill, preheat grill. Reduce heat to medium. Place steak on grill rack over heat. Cover and grill as above.)

FOUR Meanwhile, simmer reserved marinade over medium heat until reduced by half. Keep warm.

FIVE To serve, thinly slice steak diagonally across the grain. Drizzle with reduced marinade.

FREEZE AHEAD: Prepare recipe through Step Two but don't drain steak. Place steak and marinade in a freezer bag. Freeze up to 1 month. Defrost completely in refrigerator. Drain steak. Continue according to Step Three.

Pearl Couscous Salad

LARGE PEARL COUSCOUS HAS A DELIGHTFUL TEXTURE AND MAKES A BEAUTIFUL SALAD.

MAKES 10 to 12 servings

- 6 **cups dried pearl couscous, cooked according to package directions**
- 1 **cup shredded carrots**
- 1 **cup chopped green bell pepper**
- 1 **medium red onion, thinly sliced**
- ¼ **cup finely chopped fresh flat-leaf parsley**
- ½ **cup olive oil**
- ¼ **cup fresh lemon juice**
- 1 **tablespoon Dijon mustard**
- 1 **teaspoon salt (or to taste)**
- ½ **teaspoon black pepper (or to taste)**

ONE In a large bowl combine couscous, carrots, bell pepper, onion, and parsley; set aside.

TWO For dressing, in a medium bowl whisk together olive oil, lemon juice, mustard, salt, and black pepper. Pour dressing over couscous mixture; toss to coat.

THREE Serve immediately or cover and refrigerate. To serve warm, place salad in a 2-quart baking dish. Heat in a 350°F oven 20 minutes.

PLAN AHEAD: Prepare recipe through Step Two. Cover and refrigerate up to 1 day. To serve warm, preheat oven to 350°F; heat in oven 20 minutes.

Chop Chop Salad

THIS IS A FUN SALAD TO EAT! ADD CHOPPED,
COOKED CHICKEN, SHRIMP, OR TOFU TO MAKE IT A
MAIN DISH.

MAKES 12 servings

- 1 head napa cabbage, shredded
- ¾ cup sliced green onions
- 1 cup chopped or sliced red bell pepper
- ½ cup vegetable oil
- 2 tablespoons toasted sesame oil
- 2 tablespoons peanut butter
- ⅓ cup rice or red wine vinegar
- ¼ cup sugar
- 2 teaspoons soy sauce
- 2 teaspoons grated fresh ginger
- 2 15-ounce cans mandarin oranges, drained
- 2 cups honey-roasted cashews or peanuts

ONE In a large bowl combine cabbage, green onions, and bell pepper; set aside.

TWO In a small bowl whisk together vegetable oil, sesame oil, peanut butter, vinegar, sugar, soy sauce, and ginger. Pour over cabbage mixture; toss to coat. Top salad with drained mandarin oranges and cashews. Serve immediately.

PLAN AHEAD: Prepare recipe through Step One. Cover and refrigerate up to 1 day. Continue according to Step Two.

Cherry Tomato Salad

THIS IS WONDERFUL SERVED HOT, WARM, OR COLD.

MAKES 8 to 12 servings

- 1 **tablespoon chopped fresh garlic**
- ¼ **cup olive oil**
- 5 **cups cherry tomatoes**
- ¾ **cup sliced green onions or 1 cup finely chopped onions**
- ¼ **cup red wine vinegar**
- 2 **teaspoons salt**
- ½ **teaspoon black pepper**
- 1 **cup coarsely chopped fresh flat-leaf parsley**

ONE In a large skillet cook and stir garlic in hot olive oil over medium-high heat for 2 minutes. Add tomatoes and onions to skillet; cook and stir 3 to 4 minutes or until tomato skins start to burst. Stir in vinegar, salt, and pepper. Sprinkle with parsley; toss to coat. Serve immediately.

PLAN AHEAD: Prepare salad. Cover and refrigerate up to 1 day. Serve chilled or reheat over low heat.

TO SERVE COLD: Combine all ingredients. Cover and refrigerate up to 1 day.

Birthday Dinners

Young or old, we all enjoy the fun of birthday celebrations. Tie balloons on your mailbox to put guests in the party spirit as soon as they drive up. Hang small balloons and curly-ribbon streamers from the light fixture over your dining room table. Use a punch bowl and cups to add to the party atmosphere.

This menu includes recipes for special foods that are easy to prepare. They can be adapted to either a casual gathering or a dressy dinner party.

Cornish game hens make any meal fun because each person gets a whole hen. The potatoes and asparagus salad can be made ahead, and the biscuit dough is kept in the refrigerator until it's time to roll out and bake. The recipes all serve six, but can be doubled or tripled. Follow one of our ideas for personalizing a bakery cake, and this dinner is a snap!

The Party Plan

MENU
Roasted Cornish Game Hens
Cheesy Stuffed Potatoes
Asparagus Salad
Angel Biscuits
Birthday Cake or Decorated Bakery Cake

1 WEEK AHEAD
+ Plan schedule for the party.
+ Organize a Pictionary game: Write words, obtain dry-erase board and marker.
+ Grocery shop for all but perishables.
+ Mix up Angel Biscuit dough and store in refrigerator.
+ Follow freeze-ahead tip for Cornish Game Hens and Cheesy Stuffed Potatoes.

2 DAYS AHEAD
+ Set tables. Set out and label serving platters. Set out serving utensils.
+ Place frozen hens and potatoes in refrigerator to defrost.

1 DAY AHEAD
+ Purchase cake and decorate.
+ Follow plan-ahead tip for Asparagus Salad.

DAY OF PARTY
+ Roll out biscuit dough up to 4½ hours before dinner time.
+ Finish Asparagus Salad 4 hours before dinner time.
+ Begin roasting hens 1 hour before dinner time.
+ Begin baking potatoes 30 minutes before dinner time.
+ Bake biscuits 20 minutes before dinner time.

BIRTHDAY FUN
+ Play your version of the game Pictionary, using personalized words and subjects pertaining to the birthday guest.

Roasted Cornish Game Hens

CORNISH GAME HENS MAKE ANY MEAL ELEGANT BECAUSE EVERYONE GETS A WHOLE HEN.

MAKES 6 servings

Nonstick cooking spray

6 **tablespoons butter, softened**

6 **sprigs fresh rosemary, snipped**

2 **tablespoons seasoned salt**

6 **teaspoons minced fresh garlic**

6 **1¼- to 1½-pound Cornish game hens**

2 **large lemons, each sliced into 3 pieces**

2 **tablespoons olive oil**

Salt to taste

ONE Preheat oven to 375°F. Coat a large roasting pan and rack with cooking spray; set aside.

TWO In a small bowl combine butter, rosemary, seasoned salt, and garlic; set aside.

THREE Rinse the insides of hens; pat dry with paper towels. Starting at the neck of each hen use your fingers to loosen the skin from the meat, leaving skin attached at the top. Spread butter mixture evenly under the skin of each hen. Place one piece of lemon inside each hen.

FOUR Tie drumsticks to tail. Place hens, breast side up, on a rack in prepared roasting pan; twist wing tips under back. Brush hens with olive oil and sprinkle with salt.

FIVE Roast, uncovered, 45 minutes to 1 hour or until an instant-read thermometer inserted into the thigh (thermometer should not touch bone) of each hen registers 180°F and juices run clear.

SIX Arrange hens on serving platter. Drizzle with some of the pan juices.

PLAN AHEAD: Prepare recipe through Step Three but don't preheat oven or coat pan. Cover and refrigerate up to 1 day. Preheat oven. Coat pan. Continue according to Step Four.

FREEZE AHEAD: Prepare recipe through Step Three but don't preheat oven or coat pan. Cover and freeze up to 1 month. Defrost completely in refrigerator. Preheat oven. Coat pan. Continue according to Step Four.

Cheesy Stuffed Potatoes

THESE TWICE-BAKED POTATOES ARE GREAT FOR CROWDS SINCE YOU CAN MAKE LOTS UP AHEAD.

MAKES 6 servings

- **3** large russet potatoes
- **1** cup plus 6 tablespoons shredded extra-sharp cheddar cheese
- **2** tablespoons butter, softened
- **½** cup milk
- **1** teaspoon seasoned salt
- **¼** cup thinly sliced green onion

ONE Preheat oven to 375°F. Pierce potatoes in several places with a fork. Bake potatoes about 1 hour or until tender. Remove from oven, leaving oven on. Cut potatoes in half lengthwise. Use a teaspoon to carefully scoop out pulp leaving a ¼-inch shell. Place pulp in a large bowl.

TWO Mash the potato pulp with a potato masher or electric mixer on low speed. Add 1 cup of the cheese, the butter, milk, and seasoned salt; beat until smooth. Stir in green onion.

THREE Divide the potato mixture evenly among the potato shells. Place in a 2-quart baking dish.

FOUR Bake, uncovered, for 20 minutes or until light brown. Sprinkle with remaining cheese. Bake for 2 to 3 minutes more or until cheese melts.

PLAN AHEAD: Prepare recipe through Step Three; turn off oven. Cover and refrigerate up to 2 days. Preheat oven. Continue according to Step Four.

FREEZE AHEAD: Prepare recipe through Step Three; turn off oven. Cover and freeze up to 1 month. Defrost completely in refrigerator. Preheat oven. Continue according to Step Four.

Asparagus Salad

BRIGHT AND FRESH, ASPARAGUS USED TO
BE THE FIRST SIGN OF SPRING. BUT NOW
WE CAN GET IT ALL YEAR LONG.

MAKES 6 servings

- 1½ **pounds fresh asparagus, cut into ½-inch slices**
- 4 **cups boiling water**
- 4 **cups cold water**
- 1 **recipe Balsamic Italian Dressing (page 147)**
- ½ **cup shredded Parmesan cheese**

ONE Place asparagus in a large bowl. Cover with boiling water. Let sit for 60 seconds. Drain asparagus and place in a large bowl filled with cold water. Let stand until asparagus is cool; drain.

TWO Transfer asparagus to serving platter. Drizzle with dressing and sprinkle with cheese. Serve at room temperature or cover and refrigerate up to 4 hours.

PLAN AHEAD: Prepare recipe through Step One. Cover and refrigerate up to 1 week. Continue according to Step Two.

Angel Biscuits

THE DOUGH CAN BE STORED UP TO 3 WEEKS IN THE REFRIGERATOR, MAKING THIS VINTAGE RECIPE PERFECT FOR TODAY'S BUSY COOKS. SIMPLY SCOOP OUT THE AMOUNT YOU NEED AND YOU HAVE FRESH BAKED BISCUITS WITHOUT MIXING DOUGH EVERY TIME!

MAKES 16 biscuits

Nonstick cooking spray

- 5 cups flour
- 3 teaspoons baking powder
- ¼ cup sugar
- 1 teaspoon baking soda
- 1 teaspoon salt
- ¾ cup butter, softened
- 1 ¼-ounce package yeast
- ¼ cup warm water
- 2 cups buttermilk

Flour

- ½ cup butter, melted and cooled

ONE Preheat oven to 375°F. Coat a 13x9x2-inch baking dish with cooking spray; set aside.

TWO In a large bowl combine the 5 cups flour, the baking powder, sugar, baking soda, and salt. Use a pastry blender or two forks to cut in butter until mixture resembles coarse crumbs.

THREE In a small bowl dissolve yeast in warm water; add buttermilk. Make a well in the center of the flour mixture. Add buttermilk mixture. Using a fork, stir just until moistened.

FOUR Pat or lightly roll dough to ½ inch thick. Cut dough with a floured 2½-inch biscuit cutter, rerolling scraps as necessary and dipping cutter into flour between cuts. Dip each biscuit in melted butter and place in prepared baking dish. Bake 12 to 15 minutes or until golden. Remove biscuits from baking dish and serve warm.

PLAN AHEAD: Prepare recipe through Step Three but don't preheat oven or coat dish. Cover and refrigerate up to 3 weeks. Preheat oven. Coat dish. Continue according to Step Four.

Decorate a Bakery Cake

It's easy to have a personally decorated cake. Order a frosted but not decorated cake from your bakery or grocery store. Buy tubes of colored icing with decorating tips included. Look for sprinkles and other fun cake decorating supplies.

Boy's Birthday

CARS AND TRUCKS: Purchase a quarter sheet cake, frosted green. Use tubes of brown decorating icing to outline roads, filling them in with crushed chocolate cookies. Use blue decorating icing to outline a pond and fill in with blue icing. Place toy cars and trucks on the roads.

Girl's Birthday

PRINCESS CAKE: Purchase a tube cake, frosted pink. Place the legs of a 12-inch Barbie-type doll into the middle hole. Frost around the doll, and frost the doll's upper body. Use tubes of yellow, purple, and green icing to decorate the doll's cake "dress."

Adult's Birthday

CHOCOLATE CELEBRATION CAKE: Purchase a chocolate layer cake with chocolate frosting. Cover with Chocolate Shards and curly ribbon streamers. **CHOCOLATE SHARDS:** Place 2 cups chocolate chips in a medium bowl and place over a small saucepan of simmering water. Stir until smooth. Pour melted chocolate onto two 24x12-inch pieces of parchment paper or waxed paper and use an offset metal spatula to spread chocolate to cover paper, leaving a 1-inch border of paper around the edge. Place the chocolate-covered parchment on baking sheets and refrigerate until hard, about 10 minutes. Crack chocolate into shards and poke ends of shards into top and sides of cake, letting them stand up. Make 12 small curly ribbon streamers and attach each to a wooden skewer. Stick the skewers into the cake among the shards. (This cake can be made into a boy's cake by omitting the streamers and placing the action figure Hulk among the shards, as if he is exploding from the cake.)

Hors D'oeuvres Parties

A new home, anniversary, holiday gathering, christening celebration—these are just a few reasons to throw a come-and-go, finger-food type party. An open house can be fun and easy to host if you don't create too many labor-intensive foods. It helps to make only finger-foods, eliminating the need for forks. The menu should include a pleasant variety of tastes, from meat and seafood to tasty cheeses and breads. It is especially important that food for this party be make-ahead. Only final baking should need to be done the last day. And don't forget to include one or two decadent sweets.

The Party Plan

MENU
Cocoa Mocha Punch
Raspberry Punch
Ham and Turkey Finger Sandwiches
Bacon Dates
Palmiers with Honey Mustard and Prosciutto
Crab Dip Divine
Sun-Dried Tomato Dip in Party Bread Bowl
Frosted Chocolate Cookies

1 WEEK AHEAD
+ Plan music.
+ Grocery shop for all but perishables.
+ Follow freeze-ahead tip for bread bowl and freeze-ahead tip for cookies.

3 DAYS AHEAD
+ Follow plan-ahead tips for both dips.

2 DAYS AHEAD
+ Follow plan-ahead tips for Palmiers and both punches.
+ Grocery shop for perishables.

1 DAY AHEAD
+ Follow plan-ahead tip for Bacon Dates.
+ Frost cookies. Place on serving platter and cover loosely with plastic wrap.
+ Set up buffet table. Set out and label serving platters.
+ Make sure you have plenty of ice.

DAY OF PARTY
+ Defrost Party Bread Bowl. Fill with Sun-Dried Tomato Dip 3 hours before party begins; cover and refrigerate. Place on table 30 minutes before party begins.
+ Assemble the sandwiches 3 hours before party begins; place on serving platter, cover and refrigerate. Set out 20 minutes before party begins.
+ Preheat oven and bake Bacon Dates and Palmiers 45 minutes before party begins.
+ Bake Crab Dip 20 minutes before party. Fill punch bowls 15 minutes before party begins. Add ice cream to punch.

FUN FOR EVERYONE
+ Set up craft or play areas for children. The adults will be able to visit more easily, and the kids will enjoy having a fun activity.

Cocoa Mocha Punch

SERVE IN A PUNCH BOWL AND FLOAT SMALL SCOOPS OF VANILLA ICE CREAM ON TOP. AS THE ICE CREAM MELTS, IT ADDS MORE CREAMY RICHNESS.

MAKES 30 servings (2 gallons)

1 cup sugar

4 cups boiling water

1 16-ounce container chocolate syrup

1 2-ounce jar instant coffee crystals

Cold water

1 gallon milk

Vanilla ice cream

ONE In a large bowl dissolve sugar in boiling water. Stir in chocolate syrup and coffee crystals. Pour into a gallon-size container. Fill up container with cold water. Refrigerate until serving time.

TWO To serve, combine coffee mixture with milk. Transfer to serving container. Top with small scoops of ice cream.

PLAN AHEAD: Prepare recipe through Step One but don't fill container with cold water. Refrigerate up to 2 days. Add water. Continue according to Step Two.

Raspberry Punch

THE INGREDIENTS FOR THIS BRIGHT, HAPPY PUNCH CAN BE KEPT IN THE PANTRY OR FREEZER. THE PUNCH CAN BE PUT TOGETHER IN A SNAP.

MAKES 45 servings (3 gallons)

3 **quarts raspberry fruit punch**

3 **quarts cranberry juice**

2 **quarts grapefruit juice**

3 **1-liter bottles ginger ale**

ONE In a large container combine raspberry fruit punch, cranberry juice, and grapefruit juice. Cover and refrigerate at least 2 hours or until cold.

TWO To serve, combine fruit punch mixture with ginger ale.

PLAN AHEAD: Prepare recipe through Step One. Cover and refrigerate up to 2 days. Continue according to Step Two.

Bacon Dates

SWEET DATES AND SALTY BACON—ONE OF. LIFE'S PERFECT COMBINATIONS!

MAKES 24 pieces

12 slices bacon

24 pitted whole dates

ONE Preheat oven to 350°F. Bake bacon pieces on a baking sheet 10 to 15 minutes or until bacon is partially cooked but not crisp; drain off fat. Cool bacon slightly.

TWO Halve bacon slices crosswise. Wrap a piece of bacon around each date; secure each with a wooden toothpick. Place bacon-wrapped dates on baking sheet.

THREE Bake 5 to 8 minutes more or until bacon is crisp, turning once.

PLAN AHEAD: Prepare recipe through Step Two; turn off oven. Cover and refrigerate up to 1 day. Preheat oven. Continue according to Step Three.

Palmiers with Honey Mustard and Prosciutto

I'VE BEEN MAKING THESE FOR YEARS AND EVERYONE STILL FALLS AT MY FEET FOR THE RECIPE.

MAKES 3 dozen pieces

Nonstick cooking spray

½ of a 17.3-ounce package frozen puff pastry sheets, thawed (1 sheet)

Flour

¼ cup honey mustard

1 cup grated Parmesan cheese

2 ounces prosciutto, cut into thin strips

1 large egg beaten with 1 tablespoon water to make a glaze

ONE Line 2 baking sheets with parchment paper or coat with cooking spray; set aside.

TWO Unfold pastry on a lightly floured surface; roll into a 18x12-inch rectangle. Spread pastry with mustard. Sprinkle with Parmesan cheese and prosciutto. Starting at a long edge roll up pastry jelly-roll style to middle of dough. Repeat with the opposite side, making two rolls that meet in the center. Brush edges where dough meets with egg glaze; press to seal. Wrap in plastic wrap and refrigerate at least 30 minutes. Cover and refrigerate remaining egg glaze.

THREE Preheat oven to 375°F. Remove plastic wrap. Use a serrated knife to cut into ½-inch slices. Place slices on prepared baking sheets; brush tops with remaining egg glaze.

FOUR Bake 10 to 12 minutes or until puffed and light golden brown. Serve warm or at room temperature.

PLAN AHEAD: Prepare recipe through Step Two but don't prepare baking sheets. Refrigerate rolls up to 2 days. Prepare baking sheets. Continue according to Step Three.

Crab Dip Divine

THIS DIP IS ALSO DELICIOUS MADE WITH SHRIMP, SCALLOPS, LOBSTER, OR A SEAFOOD COMBINATION.

MAKES 8 cups

Nonstick cooking spray

4   **cups mayonnaise**

2   **cups shredded sharp cheddar cheese**

1   **6-ounce can crabmeat, drained, flaked, and cartilage removed**

¾   **cup sliced green onions**

½   **cup sliced, pitted black olives**

½   **cup prepared picante sauce**

1   **tablespoon chili powder**

2   **teaspoons ground cumin**

Corn chips and/or crackers

ONE Preheat oven to 350°F. Coat a 2-quart baking dish with cooking spray; set aside.

TWO In a large bowl stir together mayonnaise, cheese, crabmeat, green onions, olives, picante sauce, chili powder, and cumin. Transfer to prepared baking dish.

THREE Bake, uncovered, 12 to 15 minutes or just until heated through (don't overbake or the cheese will become oily).

FOUR Serve immediately with corn chips.

PLAN AHEAD: Prepare recipe through Step Two but don't preheat oven. Cover and refrigerate up to 3 days. Preheat oven. Continue according to Step Three.

Sun-Dried Tomato Dip

MY DEAR FRIEND PEGGY ZADINA ALWAYS HAS CLEVER RECIPES TO SHARE. THIS ONE IS GREAT AS A DIP OR AS A SANDWICH SPREAD.

MAKES 2½ cups

- 1 8-ounce package cream cheese or reduced-fat cream cheese
- ½ cup coarsely chopped sun-dried tomatoes
- ½ cup sour cream or low-fat sour cream
- ½ cup mayonnaise or reduced-fat mayonnaise
- ¾ cup finely chopped green onions
- 2 tablespoons fresh lemon juice
- 1 teaspoon seasoned salt

  Assorted crackers and/or assorted vegetable dippers

ONE In a large mixing bowl beat cream cheese, dried tomatoes, sour cream, mayonnaise, green onions, lemon juice, and seasoned salt with an electric mixer until thoroughly combined.

TWO Serve with crackers or vegetables.

PLAN AHEAD: Prepare recipe through Step One. Cover and refrigerate up to 3 days. Continue according to Step Two.

Party Bread Bowl

FILL THIS BREAD BOWL WITH DIP AND SURROUND WITH CUT-UP VEGETABLES AND CRACKERS FOR DIPPING.

MAKES 1 bowl

Nonstick cooking spray

Flour

2 **loaves frozen bread dough, thawed**

1 **large egg beaten with 1 tablespoon water to make a glaze**

1 **tablespoon kosher salt**

ONE Spray an 8- or 9-inch round cake pan with cooking spray; set aside.

TWO On a lightly floured surface knead both loaves of dough together; place in prepared pan. Let rise 30 to 45 minutes or until double in size. Carefully brush top with egg glaze; sprinkle with kosher salt.

THREE Meanwhile, preheat oven to 375°F. Bake 35 to 45 minutes or until top is dark brown. Transfer to a wire rack to cool.

FOUR Slice ½ inch off top of the bread bowl. Hollow out bowl; save insides for dipping or another use.

FREEZE AHEAD: Prepare bread bowl. Cover and freeze up to 2 weeks. Defrost completely in refrigerator.

Frosted Chocolate Cookies

DENSE AND MOIST, I'VE BEEN MAKING THE FUDGY COOKIES SINCE I WAS A NEWLYWED.

MAKES 2 dozen cookies

Nonstick cooking spray

- 1¾ **cups flour**
- 2 **teaspoons baking powder**
- ⅛ **teaspoon salt**
- ½ **cup vegetable oil**
- 1 **cup packed light brown sugar**
- 1 **large egg**
- 2 **ounces unsweetened chocolate, melted**
- 1 **teaspoon vanilla**
- ½ **cup milk**
- ½ **cup chopped pecans**
- 1 **recipe Chocolate Cookie Frosting**

ONE Preheat oven to 350°F. Coat cookie sheets with cooking spray; set aside.

TWO In a large bowl combine flour, baking powder, and salt; set aside.

THREE In a large mixing bowl beat oil, brown sugar, egg, melted chocolate, and vanilla with an electric mixer on medium speed until combined.

FOUR Gradually beat flour mixture and milk into the chocolate mixture. Stir in pecans.

FIVE Drop by slightly rounded teaspoons 2 inches apart on prepared cookie sheet. Bake 10 minutes or until edges are firm. Transfer to a wire rack; cool. Frost with Chocolate Cookie Frosting.

CHOCOLATE COOKIE FROSTING: Place 3 tablespoons butter and 2 ounces unsweetened chocolate in a saucepan. Cook and stir over low heat until melted. Gradually stir in 1½ cups powdered sugar, ¼ cup boiling water, ½ teaspoon vanilla, and ⅛ teaspoon salt. If necessary, beat in additional water to achieve desired consistency.

FREEZE AHEAD: Prepare cookies but do not frost. Place in freezer bags and freeze up to 1 month. Defrost completely in refrigerator. Frost cookies.